THE MUSEUM OF
JURASSIC TECHNOLOGY
NO ONE MAY EVER HAVE THE
SAME KNOWLEDGE AGAIN
Letters to Mt. Wilson Observatory
1915-1935
9341

Faces looking for the Future from the Past

40 possible city surfaces for the Museum of Jurassic

Technology:

WRAPPER

Robert Mangurian and Mary-Ann Ray

William Stout Publishers, San Francisco
Rice School of Architecture, Houston

Published by:
William Stout Publishers, San Francisco
and
Rice School of Architecture, Houston; Lars Lerup, Dean

Architecture at Rice 38

Distributed in North America by:
RAM Publications and Distribution
2525 Michigan Avenue, A-2
Santa Monica, CA 90404
310.453.0043
310.264.4888
e-mail: rampub@gte.net

This publication was supported by a grant from
the Graham Foundation for Advanced Studies in the Fine Arts
in conjunction with the Los Angeles Forum for Art and Architecture

'The Museum of Jurassic Technology', by Ralph Rugoff, is reprinted here with the kind permission of Ralph Rugoff from *Visual Display: Culture Beyond Appearances*, Dia Center for the Arts Discussions in Contemporary Culture Number 10, Lynne Cooke and Peter Wollen, editors, Bay Press, Seattle 1995.

Design: Studio Works, Robert Mangurian and Mary-Ann Ray
Editing: Pat Morton

ISBN 0-9651144-9-x

Library of Congress Cataloguing-in-Publication Data
is available from the publishers

Printed in Hong Kong

Contents

On the Face of It$_1$ 7
Pat Morton

On the Face of It$_2$ 8
Lars Lerup

Faces looking for the Future from the Past 10
Robert Mangurian
Mary-Ann Ray

DRAWINGS

I
Building as Container: The Ark 13
1 : ARK
2 : CONTAINER
3 : CHEST
4 : CRATE
5 : WOODEN BOX

II
Wall as Collector: John Soane in Culver City 23
6 : CASE OF DISPLAY
7 : CATALOG or COLLECTION
8 : CLAMP-ONS

III
Face as Cladding: Textile Origins of Architecture 29
9 : FRAGILE VEIL
10 : STURDY VEIL
11 : WOVEN WALL
12 : URBAN DRAPERY

IV
Inside Out: Façade as Void of Space 37
13 : INSIDE OUT

IVa
Wall as Drawing: Marks are the Thing Itself 39
13a: CAPITAL
13b: DRAWN OUT

V
Under Construction: Past the Future 43
14 : UNDER CONSTRUCTION #1
15 : UNDER CONSTRUCTION #2
16 : UNDER CONSTRUCTION #3
17 : UNDER CONSTRUCTION #4

VI
Time (and History): Clocking Buildings 51
18 : TIME PIECE #1
19 : TIME PIECE #2
20 : TIME PIECE #3

VII
Text and Words: Façade as Writing Tablet 57
21 : TEXT
22 : HIEROGLYPH
23 : SIGN

VIII
Alchemy: Surfaces of Ephemeral Substances **63**
24 : ALCHEMY
25 : ELEMENTAL CASE, or CASE OF ELEMENTS
26 : HERO'S PNEUMATICAL DOOR
27 : GUILLOTINE

IX
Fragment(s) of Technology : Stuff Gone Bad Comes Back **71**
28 : FRAG TECH
29 : HIDE TECH
30 : PATCHWORK

X
Growing Walls: Buildings as Gardens **77**
31 : HANGING GARDEN

XI
Miniature/Gigantic: Great Big and Real Small **79**
32 : CHIP CHIP
33 : MI/ACRO
34 : LARGE AS LIFE or GREAT BIG
35 : MEMNON #1
36 : MEMNON #2

XII
Recording Instruments: Measuring Buildings **89**
37 : RECORDING INSTRUMENT
38 : READOUT
39 : SHADOW CHASER

XIII
Layers: Moving In and Out **95**
40 : LAYERS OF REINHABITATION

Beyond Belief : The Museum as Metaphor **99**
Ralph Rugoff

Notes **105**
David Wilson

Essential Bibliography **110**

Acknowledgments **111**

On the Face of It[1]

Pat Morton

One of the exhibits in the Museum of Jurassic Technology documents the life and work of Geoffery Sonnabend, "a neurophysiologist and memory researcher whose three volume work *Obliscence: Theories of Forgetting and the Problem of Matter* stands a milestone in the field," in the words of the Museum's Web site. Sonnabend's theory of obliscence posits forgetting as the norm for human experience, with memory a miscognition caused by neurological dysfunction. If memory is a ruse or a constructed delusion, however, it is a necessary one for architecture. Architecture claims to resist time and its corrosive effects on memory. The physical traces of past civilizations' architecture are a valued repository of knowledge and seem to be imbued with memories of past events and lives. Even ruins represent fragments of the past that appear to embody permanence and persistence in the face of forgetting and amnesia. The collection is another hedge against forgetting. "Souvenirs," or memories collected from disparate places and times, can recall experiences that might otherwise fall into obscurity. The collection consists of objects taken out of the economic circuit and put on display. This new whole, the collection, becomes a hermetic world isolated from "real" time and space; it freezes time. Collecting is inherently a culture of fragments, a sticking together of material bits that stand as metonyms and metaphors for the world they may refer to but are not.

The use of fragments to create a new whole is predicated on the ability to efface the discrepancies between fragments, thereby creating a classification system and an ordering narrative out of the spatial juxtaposition of the fragments. This fiction requires that the fragment be detached from its context of origin and placed in a new context. If the museum conventionally gives a coherent, hierarchical narrative to history, however, the collection is often the product of a personal, surreptitious obsession. As a youth, French novelist Pierre Loti, for example, assembled a *petit musée*, a collection of seashells, birds, and anything that seemed to come from far-off lands, which he regarded as *choses troublantes*, or troubling things.

Mary-Ann Ray and Robert Mangurian's *Wrapper* is another collection, a series of forty façade studies for the Museum of Jurassic Technology. Their investigation focused on the relation of inside to outside, in particular the Museum collections to Culver City and beyond. Each plate starts with the existing façade as a base onto which Ray and Mangurian layer new façades constructed from fragments found in their own and the Museum's collections. A *tour de force* of collection itself, *Wrapper* is the Museum's correlative: a natural history of the façade.

The multitudinous façades of *Wrapper* test the unified and unifying theories of memory, collecting, and architecture. Their proliferation denies a single, coherent narrative to the Museum's façade or its history. The fragments remain distinct, while they point to other spaces and histories, other contexts. *Wrapper* is a collection that disputes architecture's status as frozen time.

The collection is a "go-between," according to Krzysztof Pomian, between the visible world of objects and the invisible world of meaning. The façade, similarly, acts as a mediator between the outside realm of appearances and the inner life of a building. A membrane of separation and permeability that belongs to both the obvious and the hidden, the façade gives a face, a visible surface, to space and habitation. It can also function as a space itself. Yet the façade disappears from memory once the building has been entered and the interior gains the upper hand over awareness. Although it seems to gird memory's fragile claim to permanence, the façade is actually another deceit. Under the influence of habit and distraction, the façade floats in and out of consciousness and, in this way, loses the face-off between memory and forgetting.

On the Face of It_2

Lars Lerup

The façade may be the architect's last resort. The interior geography, the plan and its ancient confinements and vistas, has been claimed, furrowed, indeed Balkanized by numerous others: the mortgage banker, the space planner, the marketer, the ergonomist, the interior designer, the occupant even. Façades are not without their own non-architectural claimants, including the advertiser and the semiotician. However, the nature and evolution of the façade would seem to ensure its continued alignment on the side of the architect.

The first façade may readily have been confounded with the entry - the very opening to that original cave that Umberto Eco has claimed as the beginning of his speculative spatial semiotics. A façade here is coincidental with the black hole that bridges the outside with the inside, a sign whose empty darkness promises the inner world beyond, the opening-as-mouth that, with the help of conceptual lungs, sucks the observer from the lit foreyard into the darkness of Hannah Arendt's *Oikos*.

That opening on an empty, yet promising, darkness was eventually exchanged for a "face," abstracted into a tripartite ensemble that still prevails: a beginning (at the ground), a middle, and an end where the façade meets the blue of the sky. In Europe the tripartite façade remained unchanged until the twentieth century, while in America the façade had a far looser existence. The American façade, in fact, may have begun its drift, its decline, and its disappearance as soon as the colonizers traveled west from Genoa.

A proper house, aside from its most prominent first façade, would theoretically have three others; but in America the side and the back façades soon became mere elevation, while all the householder's energies (dollars) were invested at the front. Like a grimace crossing a face, the American façade gathered and collapsed all the visible energies of the house. These cultural contortions soon were organized as veldts and vortexes around the openings (the doors, the windows) and at the edges, particularly the one at the top. Finally, words and signs were added - the writing on the wall - both sealing the itinerant fate of the façade. The decisive and intricate separation of the content of the façade from its architectonic structure (so celebrated by Le Corbusier and the Modernists in the curtain wall) was and is deceptive since it is not possible, not even in the world of images, to have content without form. Yet, once the façade was seen as a mere thinness, a sign, it didn't take long for those who claimed that its semiotic value was greater than the architectural to swiftly cut off the old face and make it a sign on the highway, leaving a crude box behind.

The assignation of such visual and ritual importance to the main façade may have supplied a built-in triggering mechanism that facilitated its own assassination. Architecture, in contradistinction to image, is predicated on built substance, while the latter depends on retinal stimulation only. Thus, the easy abandonment of the built took place in favor of any material willing and able to pull at the gaze.

The operational field of the façades still on Main Street (with all their restrictions of ground, sky, extent, and the ancient tripartite ensemble encompassing windows, doors, base, piano nobile, and corona, aside from a brief moment during Modernism and now in the hands of the few Neo-Modernists) remained, for the most part, conservative, planar, and delimited. That was the case until the façade's encounter with the proposed entry surfaces to the Museum of Jurassic Technology (MJT) by Robert Mangurian and Mary-Ann Ray of Studio Works.

To appreciate these entry surfaces may not require any special talents; however, to fully appreciate Studio Works' unusual contribution to architecture may require some deliberation. As practices go, Studio Works is highly unusual, remaining youthful and speculative because of a deep commitment to education and to research (such as digging at Hadrian's Villa for some fifteen years, not just to relive some ancient experience but to build an understanding that may be gained only by "assaying one's spade ever deeper," as was suggested by Walter Benjamin in his *Berlin Kronik*). That, combined with traditional practice, has resulted in numerous awards for unbuilt projects and to some distinguished built work. In a society where capital has long since weeded out all deep commitment to culture in favor of market freedom (i.e., predictability or annihilation), Studio Works remains highly unusual and exemplary by serving as an antidote to commercialism. In its immensely rewarding ventures, Studio Works proves that architectural culture has a wide and wondrous horizon that, even if sparely populated, still promises something greater than satisfying the profit motive.

Inspired by the very nature of the MJT (so eloquently explored below by Ralph Rugoff), Studio Works' façades - or entry surfaces - swiftly dispose of some of the salient limitations of the common façade. This is a disposal neither of the extent nor of the windows and doors, but of petrified ambitions, those restrictions on content, aspiration, and range of subject that seem to hold the façade hostage.

Studio Works' façades, in the manner of the drifting American façade, seem to have left both the vertical and the horizontal geographies of the house behind in order to stake out a new domain. First, they have a thickness perhaps akin to the baroque façade. Second, they have a scope (although still constrained by the size of the front of the MJT) that extends far beyond the façade itself.

Despite their precision, Studio Works' façades (maybe because they are so many and so varied) have a looseness, a generosity, an intended weakness that suggests heterogeneity, frivolity, abundance, even hilarity. With academic seriousness (but not academic erudition) done away with, their façades begin to foam at the mouth, to warp, expand, stutter and perform parallaxes with plans, landscapes, and entire subjects (gardens, the ark, machines, airplanes, etc.). Crazed, even stoned (*a la* Rugoff), these façades perform rather than just show themselves.

Elevational performance may have its antecedents in Robert Venturi's definition of the building "as duck," in which the entire shape performs to project a strictly extra-architectural image: the hamburger joint-*cum*-duck. At the other end of Venturi's conceptualization sits the static decorated shed in which all performative intentions have been reduced to mere inscription. Both these elevational strategies are alive and well and involved in an intense turf battle, as represented by the severely deformed "Francis Bacon duck" of Frank Gehry's Guggenheim Museum in Bilbao and by Jacques Herzog and Pierre de Meuron's decorated shed-as-library near Berlin in the town of Eberswalde. In the latter, panels cover the entire building with images by the German photographer Thomas Ruff. The building itself is a simple box. Performative exuberance thus meets the *Poesie des Ärmlichen* (Poetry of Simplicity/Poverty). An image is worth a thousands twists and turns.

Studio Works' façades refuse to embrace either of these spectral positions by mixing both - a position that may not bring fame and glory since only binary positions *in extremis* seem to achieve this. Studio Works' work is both/and, thus weak (in the sense of Gianni Vattimo and Pier Aldo Rovatti's *il pensiero debole*) in its conceptual intention rather than assertive, assured and ideological. If Gehry is Bacon and Herzog and de Meuron are the cool tattoo artists (now in uptown offices), Studio Works is Frank Stella, whose historical references to grand painting are as explicit as Studio Works' references to Mediterranean culture.

So at the one end we have Muscle Beach with a glistening, hard-pumped self-referenced body forever in tension, and at the other end we have the cool downtown body with its decorated biceps, shoulder, and ankle. Yet both may be the same body, with different aspects in focus. The only distinction between the body builder and the male model striding down the runway are degrees of class and cool.

The status of Studio Works' façades is much harder to distinguish. The exuberance and multitude of references, exacerbated by the deliberate gap between the image of the projected façade and the associated verbal description, suggests that the real façade sits in this suggestive gap. Wild, stoned if you like, these façades open rather than close, expand rather than contract, proliferate rather than reduce, scatter critically more than pinpoint. The images remind me of Max Ernst's etchings, while the written descriptions read like *Popular Mechanics*. This discrepancy, this chasm between image and word, shows not only an openness, a hesitancy at the limits of images, but that the façade has yet to find its precise location and nature in the pragmatics of construction. However, as the texts suggest, this construction process will be open to an equally wild expression in which the palette of building materials expands to include, among other things, airplane parts and plants.

In the end, these voluptuous façades float cryptically between imaginary landscapes and Max Ernst's *Les Femmes sans Têtes* (Women Without Heads), a reference which incidentally may also capture their enigmatic status: the façade is the tête on the building-as-body and Studio Works may well be trying to lose theirs, or suggest that we should lose ours.

Faces looking for the Future from the Past

40 possible city surfaces for the Museum of Jurassic Technology:

WRAPPER

Acting as architects for this project has been strange. The architecture already exists (the building stands at 9341 Venice Boulevard in Culver City, California), so who needs architecture anyway? The building is probably more intriguing than architecture; it is a building 'built' more by the things that it holds than by the walls that contain them. At various times the building will contain a working motor no larger than 1/64th of an inch, a young woman's horn, a duck's breath cure, and the life and the work of the maker of the museum. David Wilson and his collaborators are not architects, but they make the museum by the sound of an accordion; by the library that they draw from; by the back studio-office that generates, repairs, and installs the pieces of the collection; and by the continual work of making and remaking the building from the inside out through the changing collections and by the strange and dim ambiance of the displays and of the spaces between them. We were called in to remake the façade, one of the supporting surfaces, for this container building. David suggested that the work might lie somewhere between Sir John Soane's House and the Culver City vernacular.

On the first visit to the museum, the sensation of the building as a container was overwhelming. If the 'actual' architecture of the building feels like anything at all, it feels like a big wrapper for the purpose of holding the collection and for keeping the collection separate from the light of the Southern California sky. It is a building in which the contained is not controlled by the container. We found ourselves moving back (or projecting ahead) toward versions of architecture born from the imitation of containers: basketry, ceramics, and hide pouches holding liquids, food, treasured and useful things, or clothing that holds us.

Also on this first visit, coincidences of interest were noted: archaeology, collecting, the depiction of Noah's Ark (in etchings), the subtractive stone rooms of Cerveteri, Pergolesi playing, accordion, In-N-Out Burger iced tea mixed with lemonade, stuff, and an idea about making things - things that make myths, stories, and histories absolutely real because they confront us in the here and now, in absolute physical form. Many things began to sink in.

Cradling the In-N-Out Burger beverage, the drive back through Culver City led to ideas for surfaces for attachment devices telling time (made something like dingbat medallions), surfaces of text, a missing piece of surface revealing a nonexistent former state, and other deviant surfaces.

Back at the studio more associations were made: Susan Stewart's *On Longing* (especially "The Miniature," "The Collection," and "The Gigantic"), Boulee, Ledoux, Piranesi, Durand. These, along with Soane, satiated the 'real' architect in us. Other thoughts were of Hero of Alexandria's alchemical contraptions, etched and pigmented 'blueprints' on the stone walls of the Temple of Apollo at Didyma, the temporal depth of surface in the façade of a palazzo adjacent to Santo Stefano in Bologna, and the memory theater.

We set to the task of 'building' a reader to contain the associations - two working copies, one for the studio, one for the building. And we wrote down many things:

> Building Under Construction, bamboo scaffolding, Hagia Sophia filled with 1 x 2 wood, Egyptian crates, Domenico Fontana's obelisk raising, restoration; Fragile Veil, airplane wing with cloth + dope, kevlar (bulletproof truck cloth), blue tarps, hanging curtain with various drapes, bunting - America's 'dress up' buildings, stretched cloth walls - Saqqara, Bologna facade - four or five superimposed walls, magnifications of existing façades, Giotto's buildings, Minoan façade maquettes; Alchemy, Eric Orr's fire + water; Growing Wall - wall of planted bands, ancient plants - papyrus, cattails, acanthus, Roman flames, lotus, sunflower, hanging gardens of Babylon/ Masada; Wall as Drawing, geometry inscribed on wall (visible only in raking light), column in Mantova, Didyma drawings, Pantheon drawings next to the Tomb of Augustus, tools/drawing instruments, impression/imprint of a previous building left after its demolition; Miniature/Gigantic, Susan Stewart's *On Longing*, column that is mostly underground and huge, other huge elements that don't fit (running off edges), gigantic bricks and stones of painted wood/ titanium/galvanized metal, peep holes *à la* Poirier, or slots, with views into big things, full size/scale fragments of St. Peter's facade or Temple of Apollo at Didyma, head-of-pins wall; Wall as Collector,

John Soane in Culver City, shelves, frames, niches, places for attachments/hanger-ons, façade as a big glass case; Time (and history), clocks indicating various kinds of time, building as readout, MAO clock project at WSU, cranks and handles inside for adjusting/calibrating, back side of wall like being inside a clock mechanism; Recording Instrument, façade as a surface to measure exterior conditions: wind, temperature, light, air chemistry, changing scene (pinhole camera), traffic, periscope (looks at planes landing at LAX), mirror of sky/atmosphere, sounds, visitors to the museum, sundial, earth movement, readouts inside (or somewhere else); Building as Container - The Ark, etchings of the ark, seeing into display and storage places, interlocking wooden Chinese box; Fragments of Technology, something that goes bad and comes for free (salvaged tech), stealth bomber parts (unusable), carbon fiber from Jurassic period, machine-age stuff - dead tech, control panels, bricks of circuit boards (cast in resin), patchwork quilt of tech surfaces, computer chip enlarged to fill façade (MOMA catalog); Text + Words, cropped signs/letter forms, Egyptian hieroglyph, lots of words, gibberish, fragments of 100 great books or catalogs or encyclopedias, giant marquee - back-lit white plastic with changeable letters, exaggerated elements, broken frames, Giulio R. and M. Angelo, fire, water, earth, air, display windows, frames, shelves, moulding-becomes-bench, downspout, Cerveteri moulding, Piranesi, Culver City stucco color. . .

We made a careful drawing of the façade from the seismic engineer's blueprints and from some detailed measurements that we made. The project came about in the first place because the front wall needed to be structured for earthquakes. We scanned the measured drawing and printed a pile of blank (though not entirely empty) 'slates'. We trimmed these to a narrow proportion and began to build drawn proposals. The drawings were produced from used and recycled samplings of things - papers carried back from our travels to Egypt, Mexico, China, Italy, and the other side of Los Angeles; shapes, surfaces, and lines from the encyclopedias of Diderot; the printed Napoleonic editions of the Antiquities of Egypt; enlarged images of the surfaces of microprocessor chips; and things we had taken (with 35mm-fast-foto processing) from our real life, everyday, nearby and far away surroundings. This gave them a density greater than we could ever give them on our own in a short time, and we wanted to work quickly to see what would come of our almost first impressions (you have to catch them fast if you are going to catch them at all).

When we had exhausted the long list of proposals we had made in text and drawn form, we invited David to visit the studio (at that time, Studio Works was located in Howard Hughes' 1941 laboratory built to kick off the design and construction of the Spruce Goose 'flying boat'). Over an Egyptian breakfast (foul madamas, lebne with mint tea that was actually Turkish, tahina/pekmes, hummus, eggplant, honey and flat bread) we went through the pile of plates together. More coincidences of interest were noted - Susan Stewart, Hero, everyday things, Egyptian food, pre-industrial technology, Gordon Matta-Clark, Babylon . . . , and new things began to sink in.

We numbered the drawings as we went along; we had quickly devised an order for them just before David arrived. As we turned the last drawing, we hit number forty. We were pleased with the coincidence that returned us to number one, titled "Ark," and which was also the very first piece of the collection we had set our eyes upon in the first short visit. That piece of container architecture carried all the remains of culture - animal and architectural - beyond the flood. The ark left behind a grounded version of the container myth as a model for all future architecture. It was perhaps saying to us that if we stray too far again, the flood will come to clean the slate again, and cause another beginning. We were mostly pleased by the correlation between our forty pages and the period of days and nights when the ark was afloat, moving between a past and a future.

The architecture we were proposing needed to keep pace with the museum. Somehow, in order to keep up, the surface must be at the same time a new surface, an old surface, and a surface not yet made.

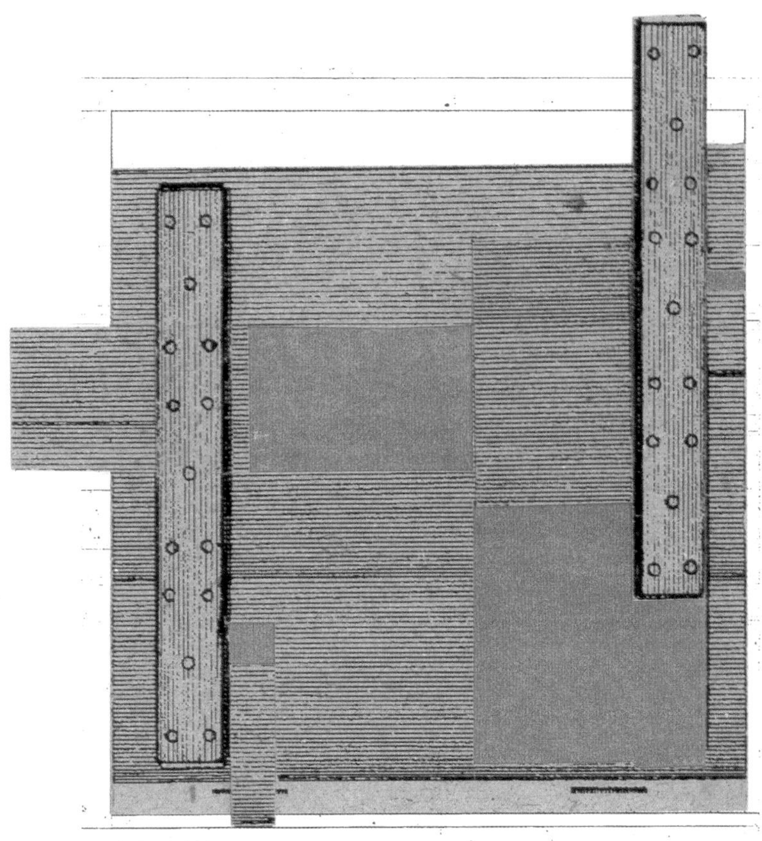

ARK
(1 : I)

Noah's Ark, a venerable artifact, suggests formal ideas and a material language. The façade of the Museum disengages from the plane of storefronts and becomes, instead, one of the short sides, or the front end, of the container-ark. The rear of the building is similarly articulated (perhaps), as well as sections of the long sides where visible. Wood is the predominant material - sheathing over ribs. Indeed this is likely one of the building's original conditions, at least on the alleyway side where wood siding remains. This construction is most evident at the entry and, again, at the party wall opening. The entry threshold could be raised so one would have to deliberately step into the container. The big container (a common vision of the Ark in the 18th century) might further have smaller containers set within it as needed: a ticketing stall, a bookstore, a storage area. These could occur in the space, now exterior, that would be captured by making the façade a single plane. The museum's existing intentional break between exterior and interior is amplified through the act of entering the hold of the ark. But this break would be quite sudden. Once within the building, the spaces would be seen as rooms within the larger container or Ark. The thickness of the Ark wall would play out the idea of the watertight wooden skin, very beautifully constructed with carefully considered detailing, attached to a structure that would seem like the hull (conceptually) of a boat. Once stepping through this thick wall (again with the thickness being occupied where possible from the inside), the collection/exhibition is protected from the 'flood' of the present.

ref: Etchings of Noah's Ark
ref: Boat construction

Sliding Box

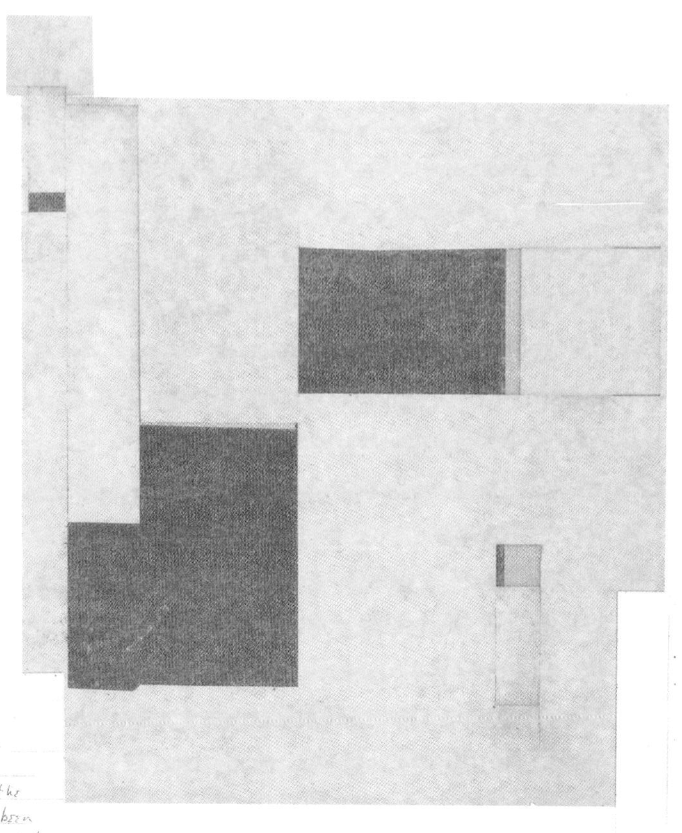

Ark —

Since our inception, the image of the Ark has been & continues to be central to The Museum of Jurassic Technology from many points of view:

— The Ark of Noah as the first & most complete museum of natural history the world has ever known. The Ark as the most complete & perfect form of the museum as an encyclopedic endeavor — one (or in this case two) of every living thing.

An institution that has been very influential in the formation of our Museum was grounded in the collecting efforts of John Tradescant who exhibited his varied & often idiosyncratic artifacts under the name of "Tradescant's Ark."

Our Museums foundation collection was donated by Mary Rose Cannon of Pasadena California. Mary Cannon indirectly received the collection from a gardener from South Platt, Nebraska who had exhibited the collections in an abandoned school-house under the name of "Thomas Ark" Noah & his wife as early, possibly the first, collectors. (In August '96, the Museum is scheduled to open an exhibition entitled "Los Angeles' Hidden Collectors" which will place in public view the collections of a number of Los Angeles area mobile home dwellers while tracing the lineage of the automobile trailer & mobile home to Noah's Ark.)

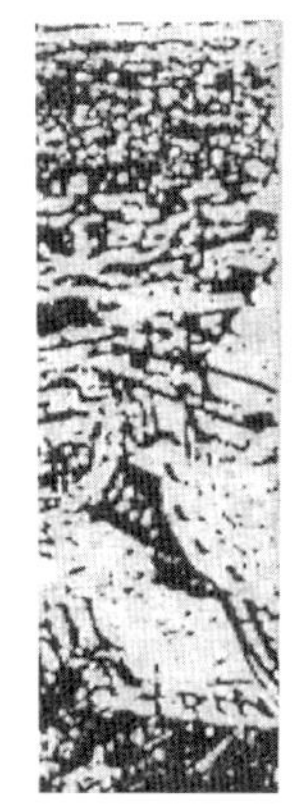

CONTAINER
(2 : I)

Another 'creation myth' within Architecture has buildings imitating those containers that were carried by people and 'people in formation' for the many hundreds of thousands of years of evolution (the first known buildings date from 300,000 years ago). These first pouches held the treasured artifacts of function and worship. The pouches transformed (in some magical way) to become buildings (containing both the people and the artifacts), but continued to exist as containers of all sorts - amphora, boxes, crates, bags, luggage, sacks, cargo container, and today's 'amphora' - the cardboard box. The building, through the transformation of the façade and entering wall, is seen as a container (quite literally) for the artifacts and the activities of The Museum. The container would be convincingly constructed of wood joined much like wood is joined in a fine container or box. Parts of the container would open (through doors to The Museum or the private second floor) or slide to access light and air from the rooms above. The container could be constructed out of teak and therefore be a container of some permanence, or out of pine and therefore signify a pine box for some decaying body. Another possibility would be the reuse of wood from some other building - perhaps wood from one of the early Howard Hughes buildings with the coloration of airplane aluminum primer.

ref: Terra Amata, Nice France
ref: Monte Testaccio

Container / Crate / Chest

Extraordinary amounts of thought, time & effort go into the creation of containers or crates for the Museum's artifacts – vibration dampening, acid free, temperature sensitive temporary homes for the objects in question. Almost mobile museums in & of themselves, the purpose of the container or crate is to protect & preserve during this a most trying & danger fraught period for any artifact — trans protection.

CHEST
(3 : I)

(see CONTAINER)

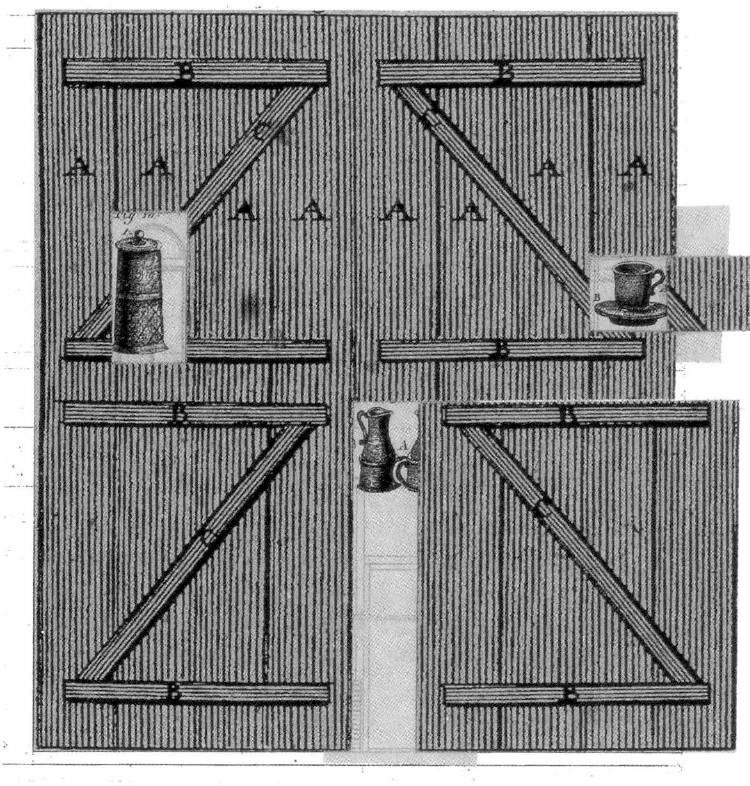

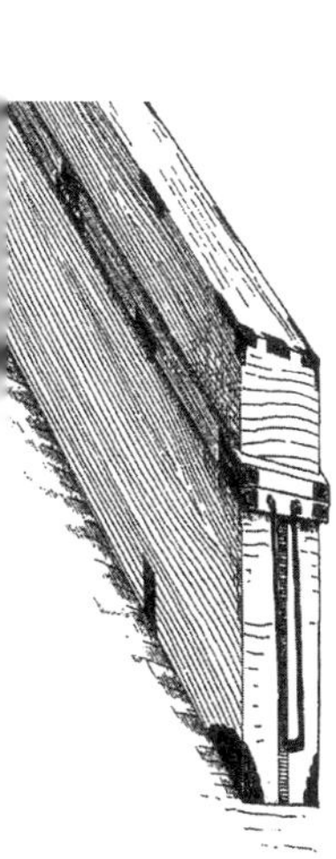

CRATE
(4 : I)

(see CONTAINER)

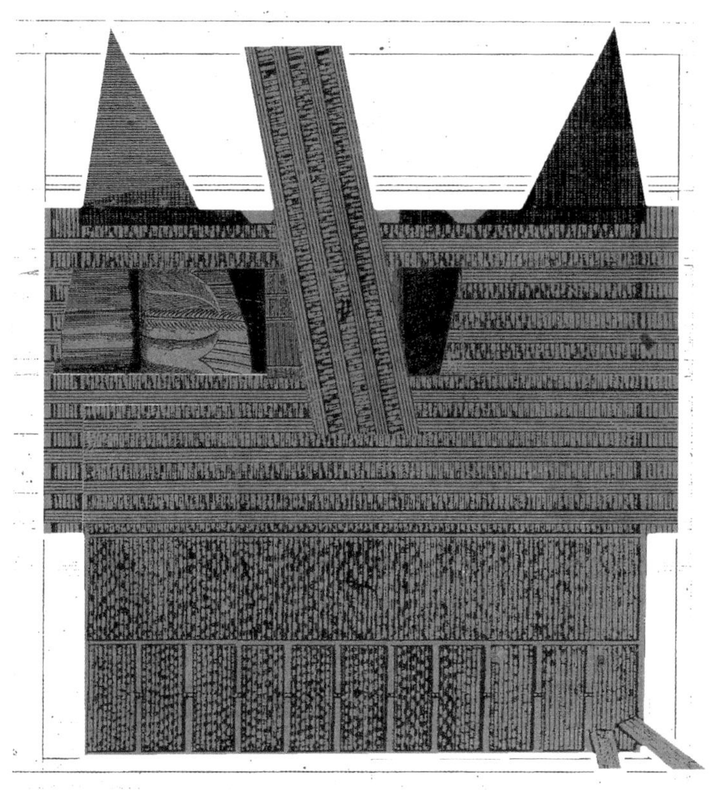

WOODEN BOX
(5 : I)

(see CONTAINER)

CASE OF DISPLAY
(6 : II)

In this wall The Museum itself becomes, and is encased in, a giant glass case. The Museum is one of the items on display behind the glass. Other artifacts would be visible, sitting on shelves, in niches, and attached to the Museum walls.

ref: Cases at the Museum of Antiquities in Cairo

Display Case

Objects change dramatically when placed under glass. Artifacts contained within vitrines are inaccessible, unreachable. Objects sequestered in such a manner are possessed of enhanced desirability – implied value. A well designed & constructed display case places the contained object in a parallel & apparently timeless reality.

State of the art display cases with light & temperature & humidity & even the constituent parts of atmosphere under precise control place the object contained in the case literally in another reality, a purer almost eternal reality where, mercifully spared from the ravages of time, objects can survive, like the incorruptibles, perhaps forever.

Cases II / Reflections

A darkened room full of internally lit display cases provides a tangle of reflection. We have greatly trained ourselves to see objects & not their reflections, however if we allow ourselves to see what is actually there, the environment is far more complex. Objects float in space while others exist in vitrines from one perspective & disappear from another — two or more objects can share the same physical space & their numbers can be multiplied infinitely. From the perspective of the museum's patrons, each of these objects, unverifiable by physical contact, is as real as the next

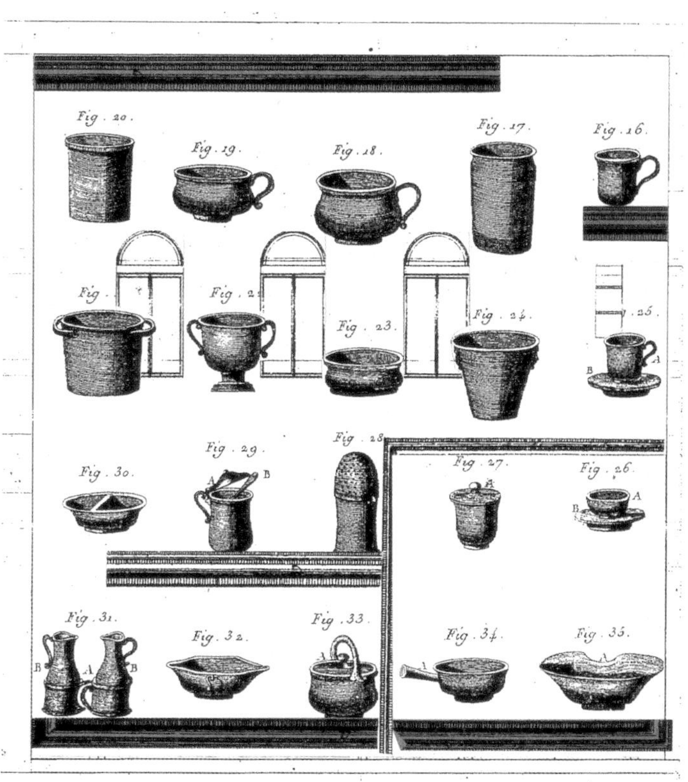

CATALOG,
or
COLLECTION
(7 : II)

CATALOG or COLLECTION follows upon the ideas of CASE OF DISPLAY and leads to CLAMP-ON. Fragments of mouldings make ledges to hold collections, to frame doors and windows, and to act as a street bench.

ref: Susan Stewart's *On Longing* - essay on collections.
ref: John Soane's house

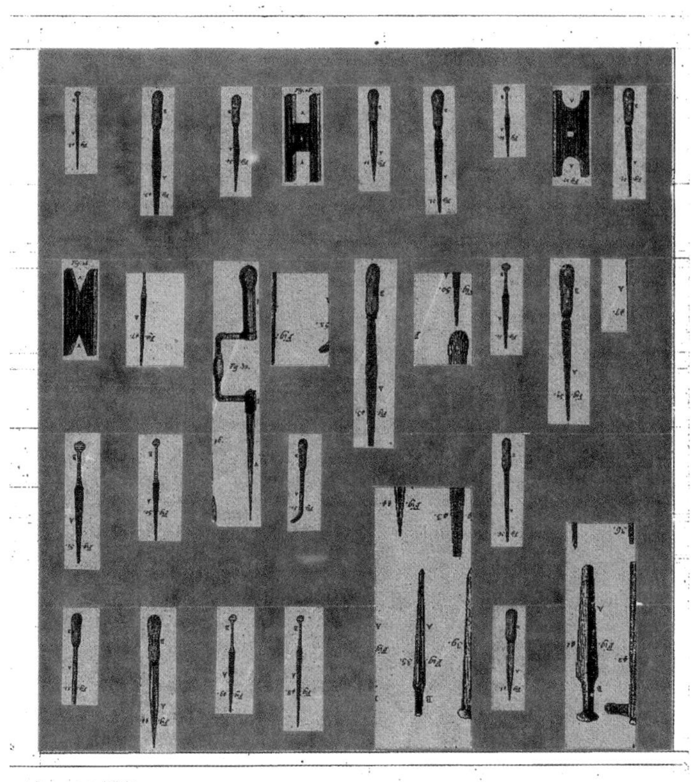

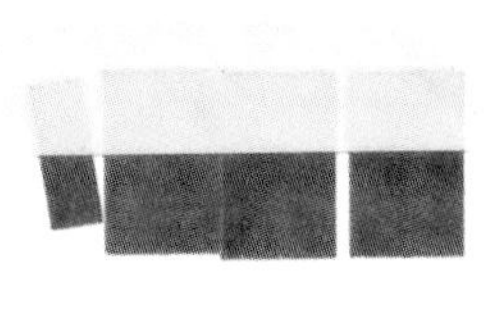

CLAMP-ONS
(8 : II)

The wall of The Museum is made of a very smooth *stucco lúcido* finish, in a radiant color akin to some of the best found in Culver City. Attached, clamped-on, outrigged to, affixed to, tacked on, appended to, tethered, harnessed, lashed, spliced, clasped, joined, and moored to this wall is a changing exhibit of various and miscellaneous collections. The outside of The Museum is a kind of transparent signal to the workings and purpose of the interior of The Museum. The workings and purpose of The Museum have seeped out of the walls and are beginning to overtake the city. This idea for a wall for The Museum takes a stance in opposition to the idea for a wall called the Ark or Container, which hides, contains, and holds the collections within the confines of its surfaces.

ref: Susan Stewart's *On Longing*-essay on collections
ref: Borges' description of the infinite catalog of things
ref: John Soane's house

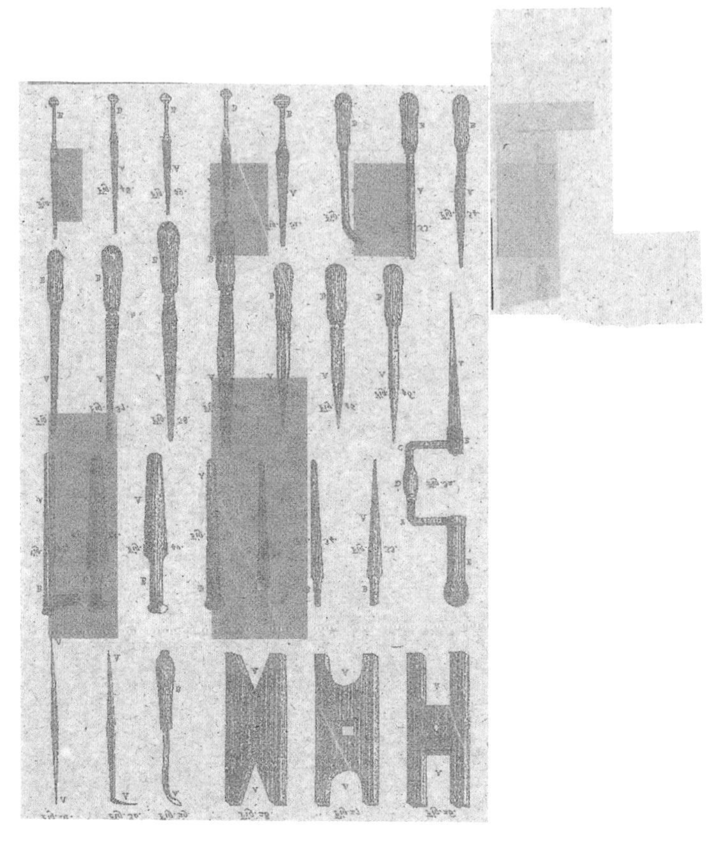

FRAGILE VEIL
(9 : III)

This wall for The Museum aligns itself to the version of the primitive hut - the origin of architecture - that theorizes that cladding (in the form of clothing) precedes structure. This wall for The Museum builds a fragile surface of fabric as a city surface or membrane. In its various versions, the material might be like the old airplanes of cloth and dope, or blue tarps, or kevlar (the bullet proof cloth used as side walls in big-rig trucks), house wrapping tents for termite treatment, something leftover from one of Christo's projects, drapes, etc. In this version, FRAGILE VEIL would be stretched on a wooden understructure, with certain elements protruding out and piercing the skin. Translucent or transparent patches would be inlaid over those areas where the upper floor windows occur.

ref: Loos and Semper's Primitive Huts
ref: B. Rudofsky's *Are Clothes Modern*, and *The Unfashionable Human Body*
ref: Shepherd's Coat, that is also a 'house'
ref: Walls at Saqqara of stone that replicate the earlier mat or cloth walled architecture
ref: 'Bunting'- early 20th century American habit of dressing up buildings with cloth swags for events

STURDY VEIL
(10 : III)

Akin to the idea of FRAGILE VEIL, the wall of STURDY VEIL would be built of a stiffer 'fabric' that could be tied about a pole, and rolled back, up, and to the sides to reveal the openings into The Museum. As would be the case in the wall of FRAGILE VEIL, the space between the veil and the wall would be extremely luminous and glowing. More openings in the walls might be made so that the glow could seep into the interior of The Museum.

Ref: Saqqara's stone doors that build a skeuomorph version of rolled and tied mat doors
Ref: Luminosity of Japanese lantern

WOVEN WALL

(11 : III)

Like a big loom, the wall structure for The Museum holds a woven surface between the inside and the outside. Moving from the city through this 'piece of fabric in the making' into the interior is like stepping into the shelter of a garment. Woven into the fabric would be the words: 'The Museum of Jurassic Technology'. Changing text could be hung on the armature of the looms rods or pinned to the body of the big cloth. The strands of the fabric could range from silk, cotton, wool to copper, silver, gold.

ref: Catal Huyuk - the first (known) city - has woven walls
ref: Terra Amata - the first (known) building - has woven walls
ref: Saqqara's stone walls replicating taut fabric stretched on poles
ref: *Women's Work - the First 2,000 Years*, the history of weaving and its connection to architecture

VP
VP

VP

URBAN DRAPERY
(12 : III)

A domestic material - the curtain or the drapery - frames and covers the wall for The Museum. It carries connotations of intimate interior spaces like the boudoir or private sitting room and connotations of the proscenium of a stage. The drapery is able to be pulled back and tied in various configurations, and may be closed during intermissions, curtain calls, times of privacy.

ref: Diderot's Encyclopedia - theater section

INSIDE OUT
(13 : IV)

The wall is rendered to suggest that it is the remaining interior wall of a building that no longer exists, whose interior space would have been where the sidewalk, and Venice Boulevard now are. INSIDE OUT wall is seen regularly in cities where the demolition of buildings takes place. Party walls often reveal traces of stairways, wallpaper, rooms painted different colors, and plumbing lines. The illusion is suggested here by traces of cut-through walls proud of the façade, and by a variety of interior details of construction: window sills, abstractions of interior light fixtures, framed paintings or mirrors hanging on the wall, wainscoting, etc. The former second floor, retaining its joists and floorboards, might protrude from the façade enough to make a kind of entry canopy. The surface finish could be smooth plaster, and some details like curtains or drapes could also be made in plaster, recalling the stone fabrics of Saqqara. The participant, on the street or in the car, would be given the impression (just for a split second) of being within, instead of being outside, the container of the artifact.

ref: Photographs of projects under demolition
ref: Michaelangelo's Laurentian Library entry space, with the trace of the previous stair left on the wall behind and to the right of his new stair

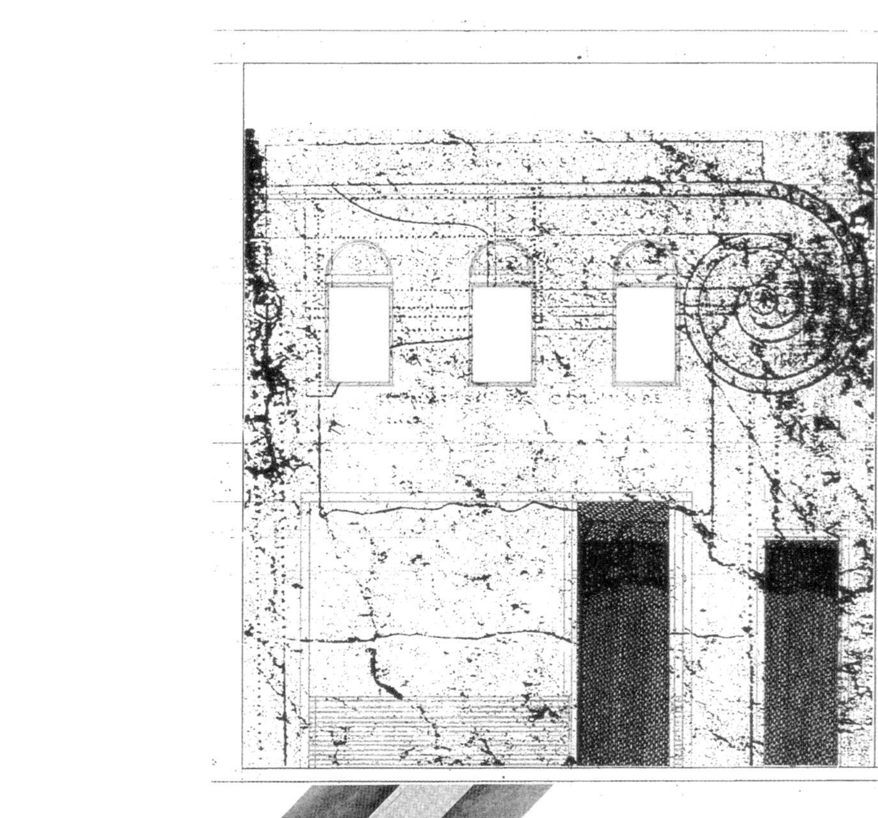

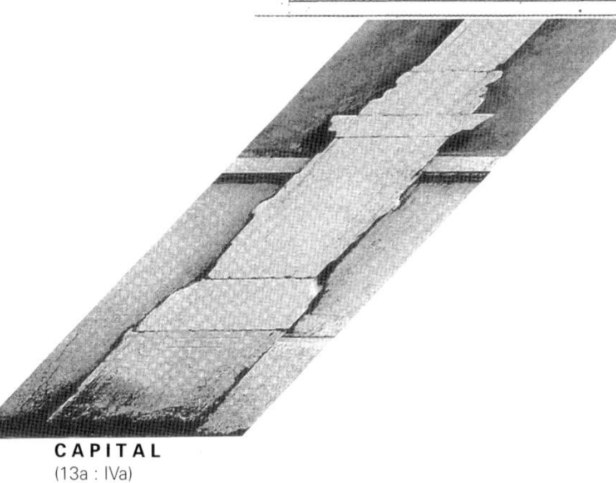

CAPITAL
(13a : IVa)

The façade is taut as a sheet of paper. But it also has mass. In the morning, before the sun heats it up, it is cool and damp - alabaster white. Parts of it are polished through use, other parts through artifice. Still other parts are coarse, unfinished: marks from the rough tool remain. Other marks, the artisan's, become the thing itself. An image of a huge capital rises from the ground, iterating the façade as a type of drawing, a construction whose controlling lines remain visible in just the right lighting conditions. An underlying order, and its derivation, is expressed: the wall is not built, only drawn. The lines are etched into the wall less than .1mm and are usually invisible. The facade is also the fragment displayed but, shown at full scale, one whose whole is gigantic, subterranean, and mostly missing. The spectator, seen against the scene, provides the scale of the real or makes the real surreal.

ref: Temple of Apollo at Didyma - drawings of column profiles on the inner walls
ref: Drawing of the Pantheon pediment in the Tomb of Augustus pavement
ref: Mantova - student of Giulio Romano (photograph) façade detail

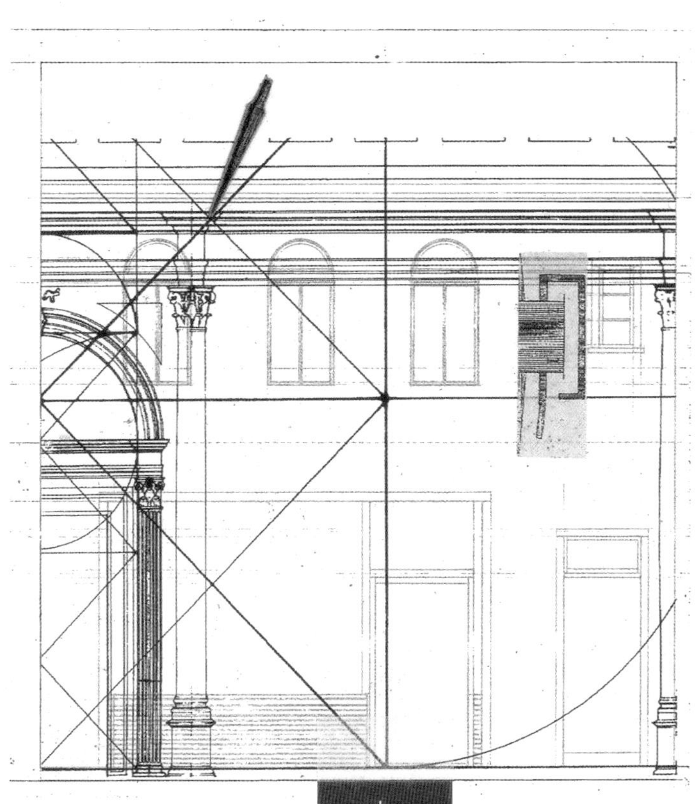

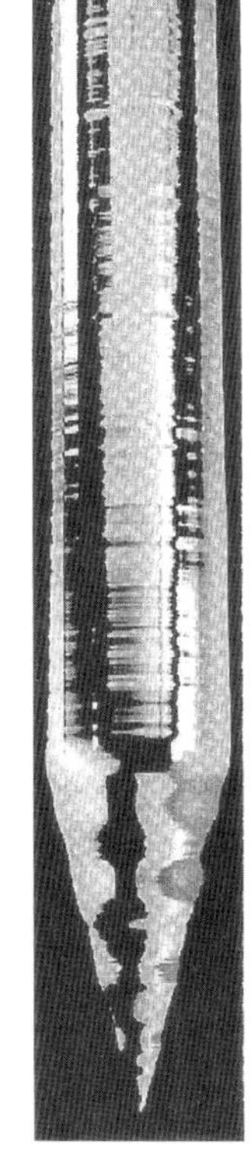

DRAWN OUT
(13b : IVa)

DRAWN OUT is never really built. Rather, its drawing is transposed directly onto the building wall. The wall of the building is prepared much like a canvas or drawing paper on a draftsperson's drawing table. The material for this drawing surface might be as simple as plywood with a white plaster-like coating (perhaps with marble dust). The seams of the plywood would be apparent, but quite subtle. The drawing will be transposed quite carefully, perhaps by laser technology, but more likely by large 'drawing/etching' instruments constructed just for this purpose. The process of drawing the 'façade' will become part of the wall. Guide lines, regulating lines, and proportional systems that are necessary to achieve the drawing will be left as a 'watermark' on the wall. Inside, we would expect to find the tools that were used to construct (draw) the wall housed in containers (instrument boxes) on the second side of the wall. These will include plumb bobs, scribing tools, large nails, wires stretched and electrically heated to sear lines into the surface, etc. All of architecture's proportional systems will be included, a kind of museum of geometry.

ref: Temple of Apollo at Didyma - drawings of column profiles on the inner walls
ref: Drawing of the Pantheon pediment in the Tomb of Augustus pavement
ref: Mantova - student of Giulio Romano (photograph) façade detail

UNDER CONSTRUCTION, or PAST THE FUTURE #1
(14 : V)

Fixed in suspended time, this wall for The Museum would be a wall constantly under construction, a wall constantly undergoing restoration, and a wall caught in the process of demolition. Simultaneously, The Museum is a building being created, a building being brought back to life, and a building facing the end of its existence. The wall of The Museum would be sheathed with the 'unsheathed' architecture of building processes: falsework, scaffolding, support braces, buttressing, cranes, unsheathed structure, framing, trestlework, platforms, etc. The Museum would be entered through the thickness of this architecture - the architecture of a building moving either toward a future or into a past - setting the stage for the multiple paths of chronologies exhibited and threaded through the collections of The Museum.

ref: Robert Smithson's *Hotel Palenque*
ref: Hagia Sophia filled with 1 x 2 wood scaffolding
ref: Egyptian crates
ref: Domenico Fontana's Obelisk raising (St. Peters)
ref: Bamboo scaffolding of Asia

Worn out/Under construction

— The task of providing to the world a museum w/ minimal staff & a few often desperate if desperately dedicated volunteers is at times overwhelming. New exhibitions, expanded programs & space renovation are always in the works. Exhibits, many of which employ early 20th or even 19th century technologies have on more than one occasion broken down.

The Museum's exhibitions regularly take longer (often much longer) than anticipated opening dates are repeatedly pushed back, & finally when opened, certain exhibits within the larger exhibition invariably will be posted w/ the Museum's all too familiar & well worn "Exhibit Under Construction" signage

UNDER CONSTRUCTION, or PAST THE FUTURE #2
(15 : V)

(see UNDER CONSTRUCTION or PAST THE FUTURE #1)

16
I

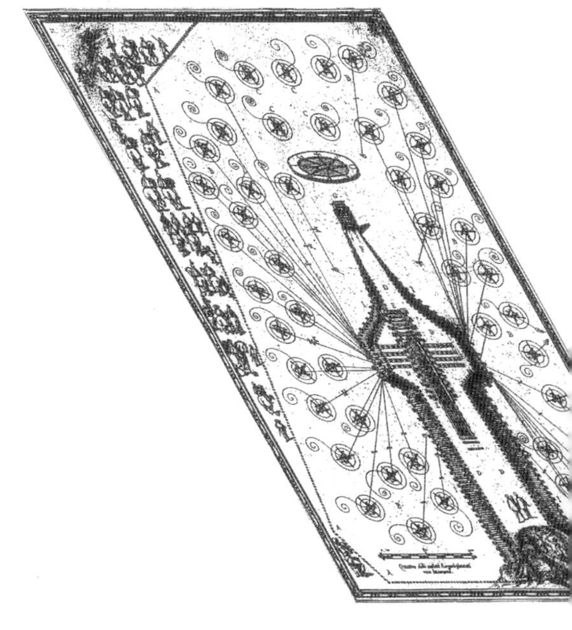

UNDER CONSTRUCTION, or PAST THE FUTURE #3
(16 : V)

(see UNDER CONSTRUCTION or PAST THE FUTURE #1)

U N D E R
C O N S T R U C T I O N,
o r
P A S T T H E F U T U R E
#4
(17 : V)

(see UNDER CONSTRUCTION or
PAST THE FUTURE #1)

Time +

1. clocks indicating kinds of time.
2. Building as readout
3. Vito, Ren, Sam
4. counters inside the clocks. – facade = like a clock.

varion

look projection.
set/reset

TIME PIECE
#1
(18 : VI)

Time Piece —

Like similar institutions, The Museum of Jurassic Technology itself is a space where standard understandings of time do not apply. It is a place where the past repeats itself over & over – a place where Bernard Maston will time after time succumb to the ravages of influenza – where Geoffrey Sonnabend will again & again be struck w/ the insight that will lead to his "Obliscence: Theories of Forgetting & the Problem of Matter" – where Madalena Delani will die hundreds or possibly thousands of untimely deaths in a freak automobile accident while on her way to catch the ferry from Buenos Aires to Montevideo.

TIME PIECE
#2
(19 : VI)

Cooper Union tower
too

Up Inside Big
Clock - Cinema
Image

TIME PIECE
#3
(20 : VI)

TEXT
(21 : VII)

Much of architecture's history has seen the building wall as a surface for telling stories. 3,000 years of Egyptian architecture saw the surface of the building as a place to write on. The texture of the surface was text. This was also true in Greek architecture, with the story telling taking place within the pediment (the façade side of the building) and within the frieze. Gothic architecture saw the building's surfaces (especially the primary surface of the façade) as a place to 'write' the story. In the modern city, the dominant visual effect is that of literal signs, with the words and images telling the stories of culture's producers and products. TEXT sees the wall of The Museum as a surface that is written on - a marquee, a page from a book, a graffiti, a sign. The problem with the text is what to say. TEXT could be merely lines of letters randomly chosen but beautifully made (letter forms are clearly some of our best designs), forming words with no meaning, words of accidental meaning, words of future or past meaning, etc. Each line could use a different type style. The words could be fragments from the texts of the 100 'great books.' The words could be randomly chosen from the front page of the *Los Angeles Times* on the day that the wall of text is constructed. The words could be in braille, or in languages no longer used or understood, or in languages that are about some future time. The words could be in some coded system, perhaps made up of the ons and offs of the 'upstart' binary code. This binary code could translate into an electronic façade that would have constantly changing messages, perhaps hooked up to a computer within The Museum.

ref: Egyptian walls
ref: Venturi's *Learning from Las Vegas*

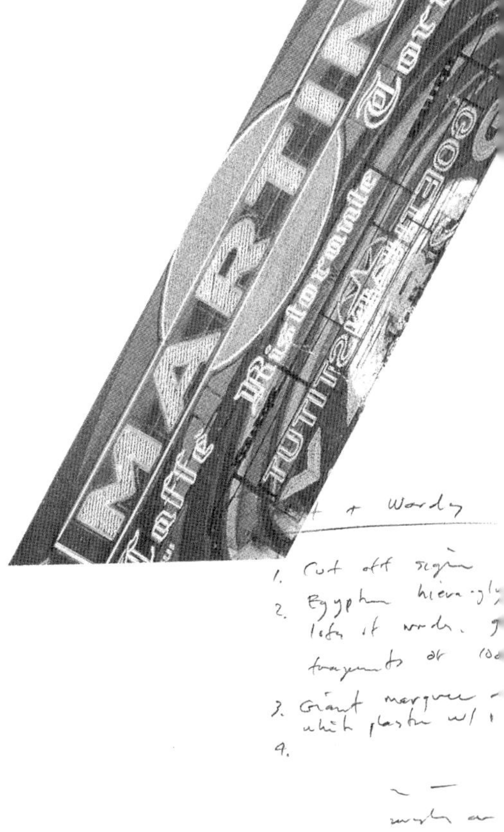

Text —

The Museum of Jurassic Technology, perhaps more than most institutions, relies on text as a means of sharing what we consider to be indispensable information w/ patrons & visitors to the Museum.

In earlier days, nearly all of the information accompanying the exhibits was presented by means of text panels. Certain of the Museum's walls became dense w/ panels of text. Patrons would read through lengthy descriptions & narratives often shifting from one foot to the other to ease the strain of standing for long periods of time required for reading. Benches were provided in hopes of easing the patrons strain; still there came a time when it was clearly untenable to continue to ask patrons, many of whom simply wander into the Museum off the street, to commit to the amount of reading required to follow the substance of the often complex exhibitions.

Other modes of presenting narratives & descriptions were sought — various forms of recorded presentation including telephone hand-sets & audio-visual offering. These newer recorded forms of presentation proved to be quite effective — effective not only in providing the Museum's patrons w/ less labor intensive means of receiving knowledge but effective, in addition, in freeing up valuable wall space within our limited domain for the ever growing body of exhibit materials.

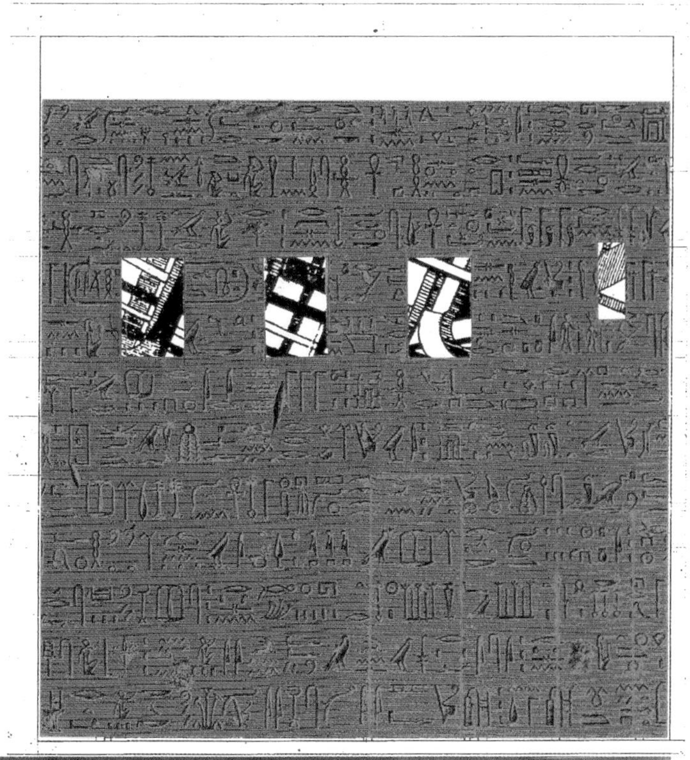

HIEROGLYPH
(22 : VII)

(see TEXT)

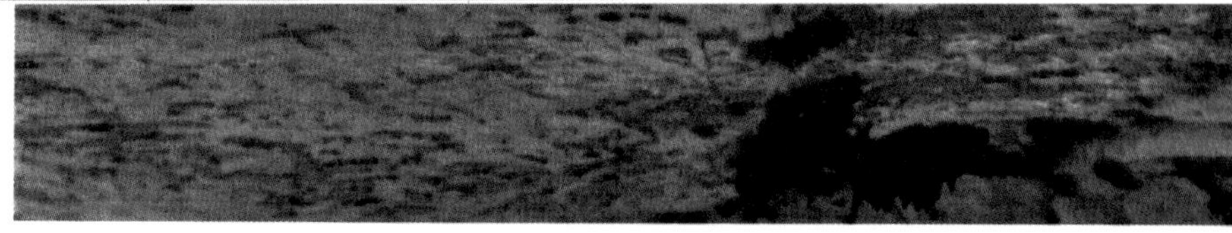

SIGN
(23 : VII)

(see TEXT)

ALCHEMY
(24 : VIII)

ALCHEMY is a wall of slatted wood (teak or other water tolerant wood) where water falls down, against and intertwined with fire that rises up. Technically, this could be realized through a collaboration with artist Eric Orr, with gas fired jets. If, on the other hand, the city building department would not allow the actual fire, a 'false' or 'simulated' fire might be made with fluorescent red paint on the undersides of the slats that would reflect down upon the adjacent slat in a fiery glow. The alchemic wall could be 'tuned' and regulated to mix fire and water at certain times of day/night, or to run 'pure' water or 'pure' fire at other times. In the alchemical mode, it might be good to throw in some gold and some base metals, which might also be visually mixed or separated out into purified states. Some slots in the wall might be inlaid glass vials with labels claiming contents of universal solvents and elixirs of life.

ref: Eric Orr's works (thank you Eric)
ref: Alchemical Formulae

Eric Orr

fire + water, wood (teak)

VIII

25
VIII

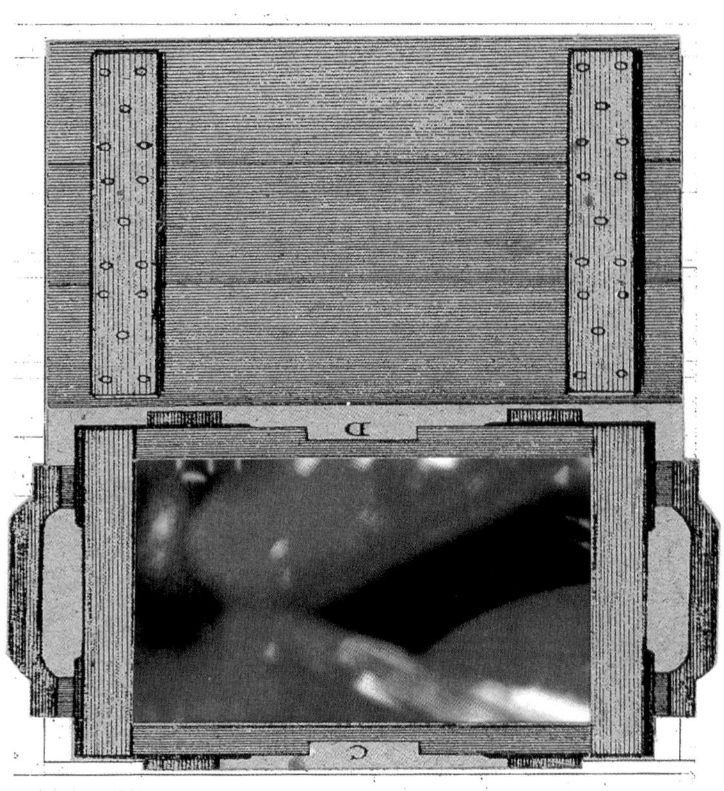

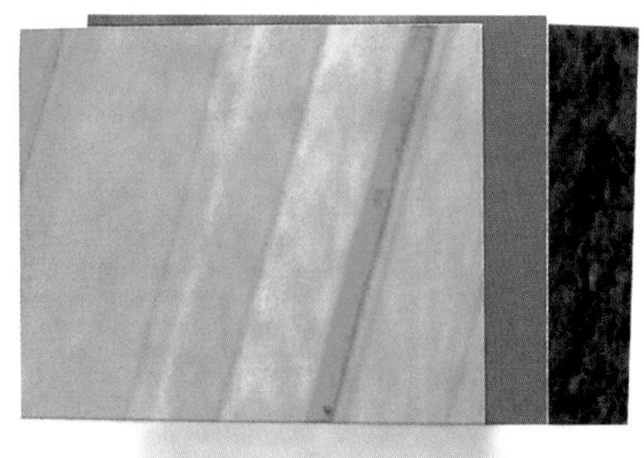

ELEMENTAL CASE,
or
CASE OF ELEMENTS
(25 : VIII)

Like an opened case or valise, the city wall of The Museum appears with a hinged open lid at the top and an empty compartment at the bottom. The purpose of the case would be to hold and display the elements of earth, air, fire, and water. By means of projections or manual inserts, the elements - or any single element - would be made to fill the empty compartment. Other artifacts could also fill the interior of the opened case, especially at times when The Museum found itself overcrowded or brimming over with things. The space inside the empty valise might also be the place where exhibits moving in or out of The Museum are un-crated and crated.

ref: Dante's *Divine Comedy*
ref: Marcel Duchamp's Cases and Valise

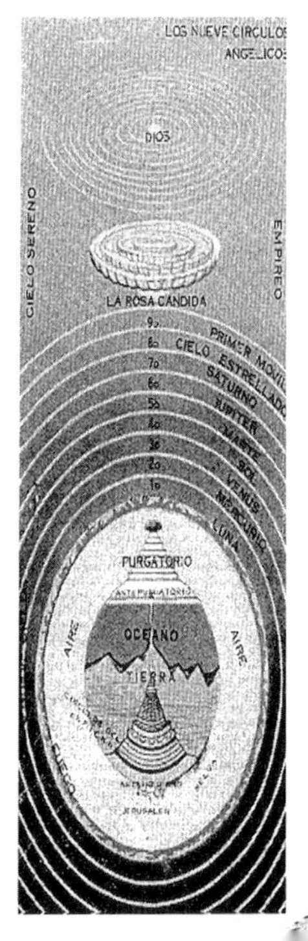

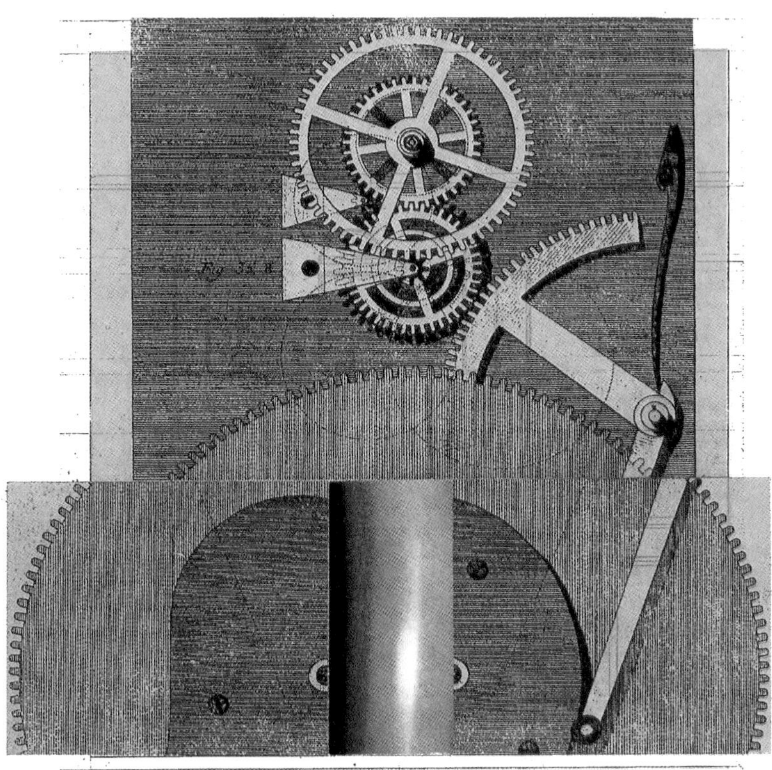

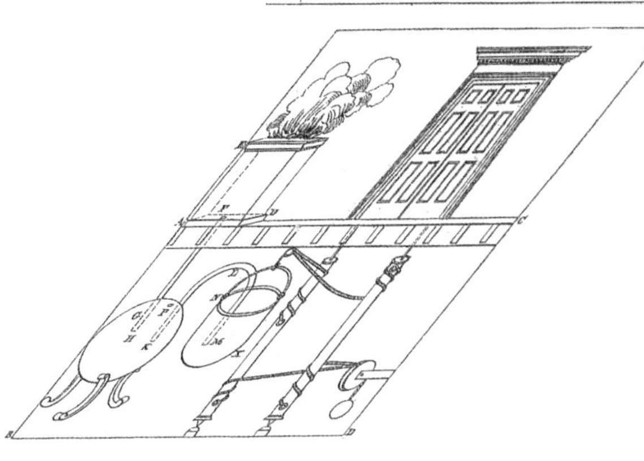

HERO'S PNEUMATICAL DOOR
(26 : VIII)

Based upon Hero of Alexandria's invention for 'Temple Doors opened by Fire on an Altar'; the front wall of The Museum might be fabricated as a reconstruction and exhibit of this mechanism. The exterior wall, in this case, would expose the ropes, pulleys, and gears involved with the mechanical parting of the doors - letting the city dweller and passerby 'in' on the secret. Large panels of the wall would slide to each side, revealing a crevice by which the interior of The Museum would be broached. The most intricate and delicate secrets of the mechanism might remain hidden: the tube, the globe, the siphon, the liquid quicksilver, the rarefied air, and the sliding leather bag. These most intricate and delicate secrets might be slowly revealed over great periods of time, to be known only to the most persistent and habitual Museum-goers.

ref: Hero of Alexandria's Treatise on Pneumatics
ref: Temple devices at Agrigento
ref: Rube Goldberg contraptions
ref: Miniature golf

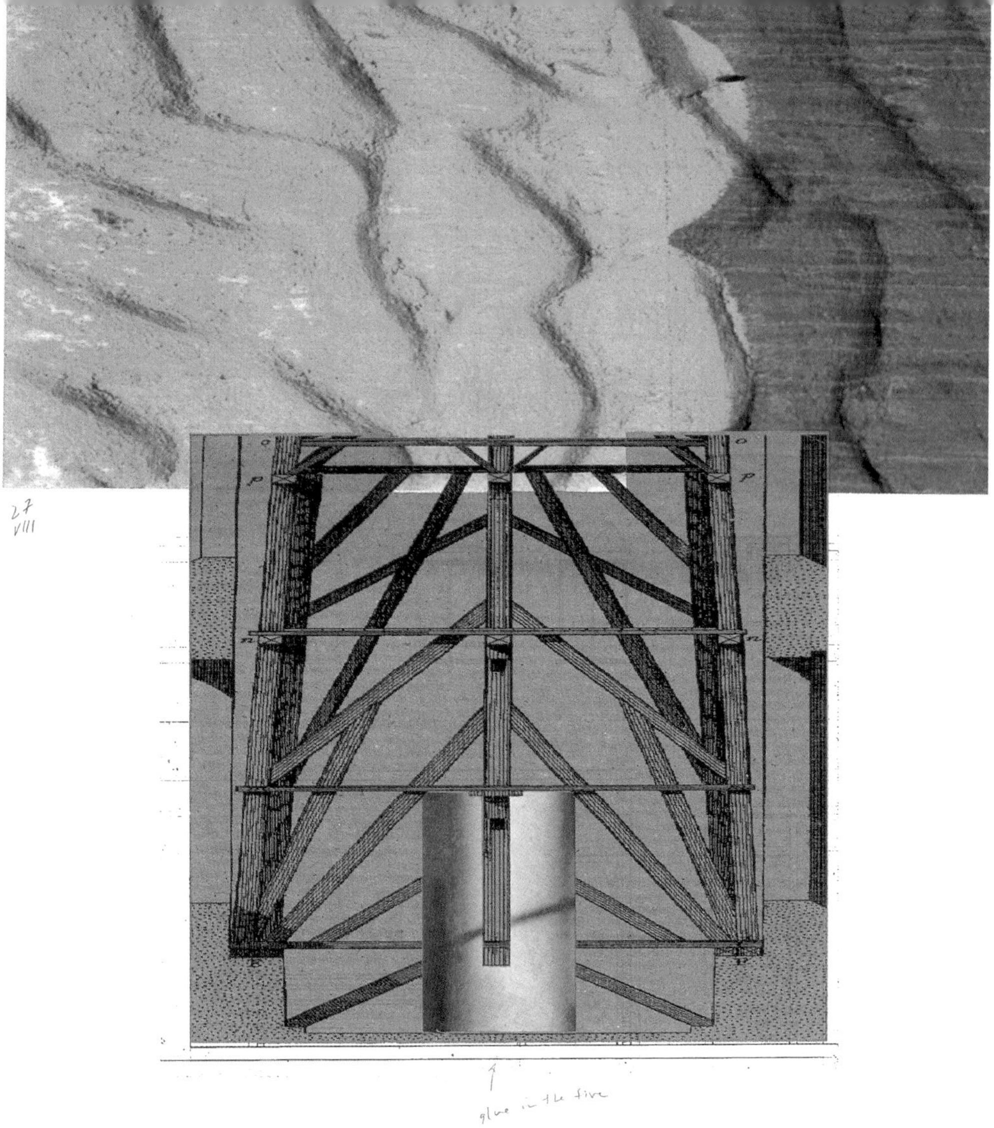

GUILLOTINE
(27 : VIII)

A mechanism for raising and lowering the door to The Museum.

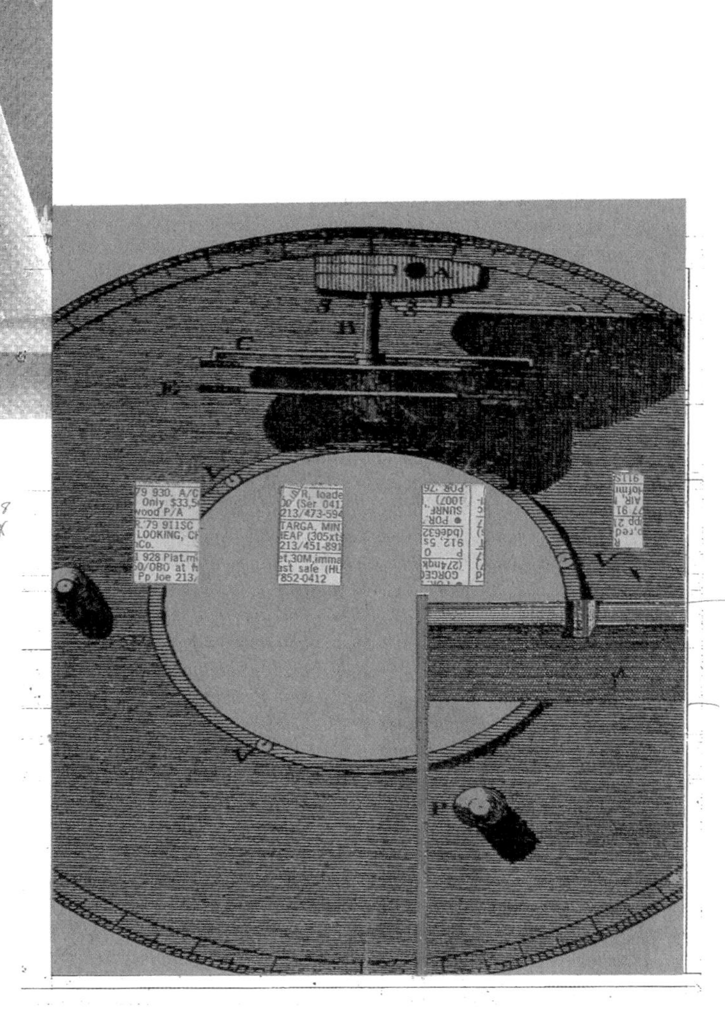

FRAG TECH
(28 : IV)

Technology and production have produced large scale constructions that finally out-last their utility or are constructed in a faulty way and must be discarded. These range from small scale to large scale. FRAG TECH attempts to capitalize on this by searching for these parts as the large scale surface element of The Museum wall. An ideal part might be a 'discarded' wing section from a 747 or C130. 'Filleting' the tail section of the 747 might produce the entire surface of 9341 Venice Boulevard. The juxtaposition of scales - part of an airplane wing to the neighboring façades - might prove useful. Other possibilities include a wall made of six very flattened car bodies, three stacked sides of a railroad freight car, large concrete sections from an abandoned freeway, or a piece of a decommissioned nuclear energy plant. FRAG TECH depends on the found part occupying most of the area of the façade. The installation of the part would be an event (perhaps brought to the site by helicopter), and documented in detail.

ref: Stealth and Space Shuttle reject parts
ref: Airplane grave yards
ref: Auto junk yards
ref: Abandoned industrial sites

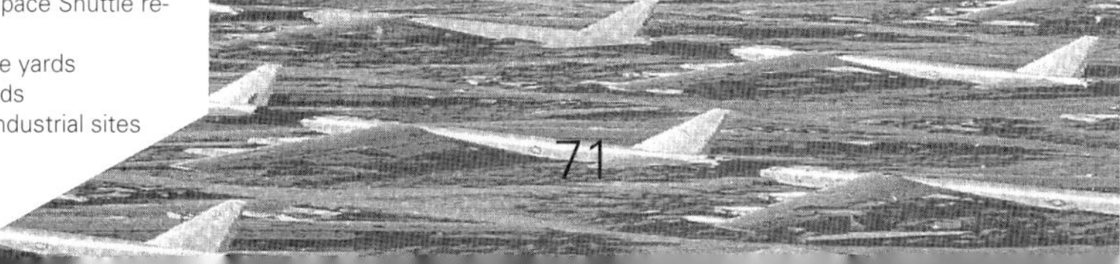

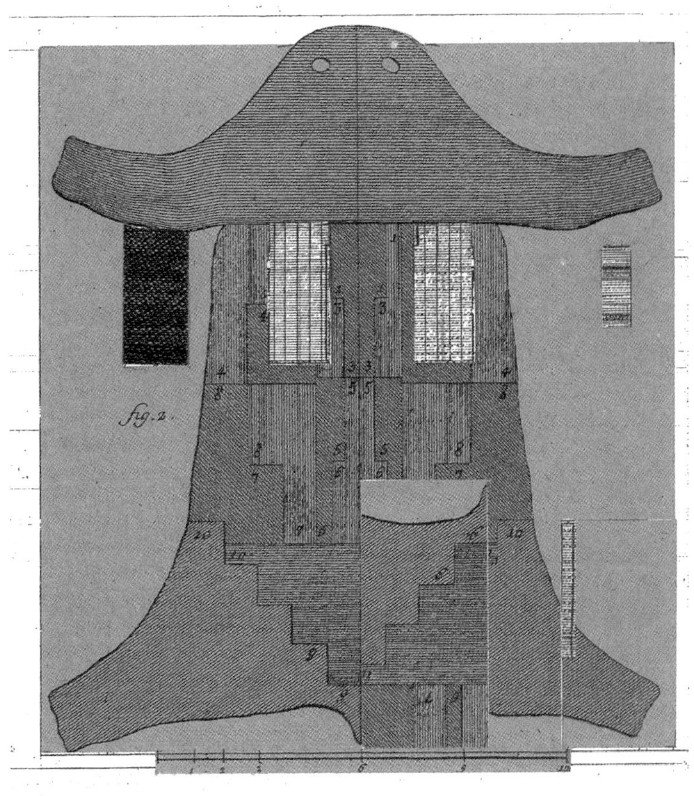

HIDE TECH

(29 : IV)

An artifact of 'technology' applied to the façade becomes a reified frame of reference. HIDE TECH marks a physical point of entry into the museum's many-framed investigation of technology and its relations to human activity. The artifact could be fragmentary or complete and might have a primary reading like 'advanced technology' or 'primitive' and 'dead'. Additionally, the piece or collection of parts might have inherent physical qualities of color, texture, pattern and form that make it an evocative surfacing material. A shape would be formed that would be unrelated to the meaning of the original use and function. The shape would evoke something quite distant in relationship to time and use of the original. Thus, some reject parts from the Stealth Bomber (carbon-fiber parts that don't meet the standards required due to some failure in lamination and/or autoclave 'baking') might be 'sewn' together to form the large hide from some mythic prehistoric creature (whose body perhaps is to be found within the carbon fibers). One of architecture's 'creation myths' posits the first building as a laying of clothing skin on a makeshift structure (Loos).

ref: B2 Bomber reject parts
ref: Animal hides - skins of living things flattened

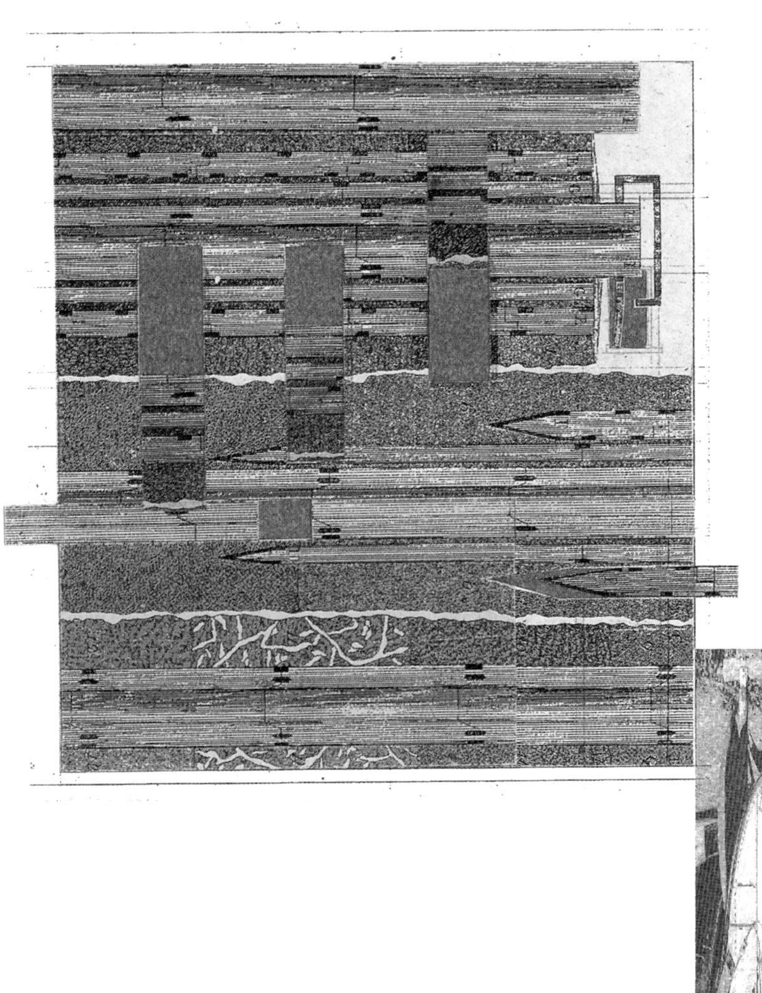

PATCHWORK
(30 : IV)

PATCHWORK stealthily searches for parts and, much like the American tradition of making blankets from fragments of cloth, pieces together discarded or rejected parts from industry. The lines of like parts form strata from industry of the 20th century. One can imagine lines of car windshields, lines of car bumpers vertically arrayed, lines of coke and beer bottles (something akin to amphora vault filler in Roman times), lines of machine parts, lines of silicone wafers and circuit boards, lines of TV sets, lines of IBM 8086 computers (selling for $7 each at aerospace industry auctions), lines of old doors from torn down buildings, lines of discarded shoes (perhaps metalized), lines of long playing records and cassette tapes, lines of auto tires, lines of industry desks (selling for $5 at auction), lines of air conditioners stacked to form the wall of The Museum. The wall would piece together these parts so as to make their original purpose and meaning quite visible. The strata would be as intriguing as the strata one finds cutting into the earth's surface through layers of the earth's 'dirt'.

ref: Auto junkyards
ref: Airplane graveyards
ref: Industrial salvage yards

Dear Robert & Mary Ann—

Here is the second installment. Let me know if there are problems w/ these.

I have some thoughts about possible ways of proceeding that I will write up & fax you.

Hope all is well.

[illegible signature]

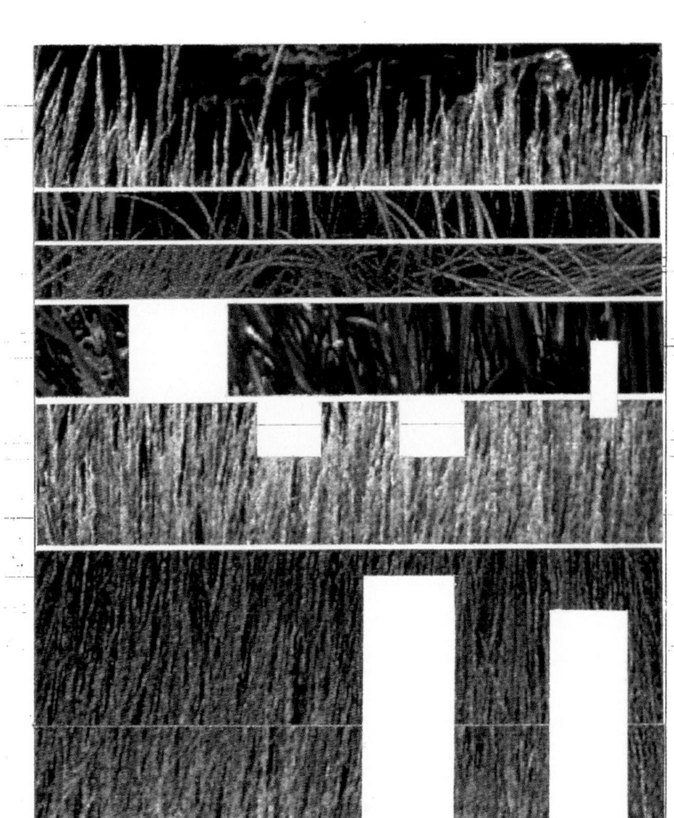

HANGING GARDEN
(31 : X)

Here, a series of long, thin, window box-like containers stratify the façade. At each level a different type of plant grows. One grouping could include those plants identified with antiquity, either generally, or because of specific historical developments in the language of architecture (papyrus in Egypt, acanthus in Greece, with Wright's hollyhock serving as a modern counterpart). Another model is Alberti's stratified, didactic façade of the Rucellai or the façade of the Colosseum with the layers of the orders of the columns. Didacticism would likely be appropriate: written descriptions of the plants and their relationships could appear within the façade (on the inside of the building). These descriptions become the first of the museum's exhibits. An altogether different time-scale, the geologic, could likewise be explored through a different selection of plants, ones whose evolutionary history particularly involved the Jurassic period. Another focus could be on agriculture as one of the earliest technologies. The watering system for such a façade, and any other of its functional requirements, would be expressed emphasizing the cyclical, the elemental, the physical: a cooling spray, the sound of dripping water, a sun break. Perhaps some of the plants are aromatic. The plants change with the seasons; thus, the colors, textures, and amount of growth cause the surface to change drastically throughout the year. The mechanisms for the maintenance of the façade (the plants) would be part of the wall. The façade begins to suggest an oasis.

ref: Hanging Gardens of Babylon
ref: Nurseries, where plants are arrayed in rows

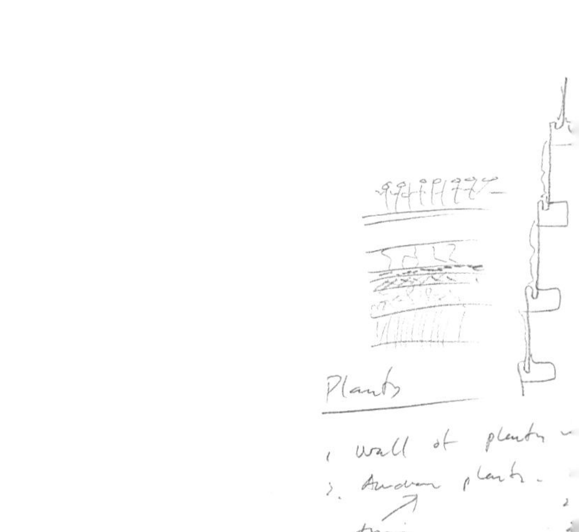

XI

32
XI

CHIP CHIP
(32 : XI)

CHIP CHIP is an enlargement of a Pentium chip (perhaps paid for by Bill Gates) that might be an actual working model. The process of making chips involves making very large drawings that get reduced to postage stamp size. Millions of transistors and circuitry, just visible to the eye, become invisible. The wall would be a further enlargement of the drawing, rather than reduction. Construction might be in panels of wood or plaster (or better yet silicone/resin or titanium) that would have the drawing etched onto the surface. The etched lines could be filled with copper or silver. The panels would be joined and attached to a substructure.

ref: MOMA Catalog of computer chips

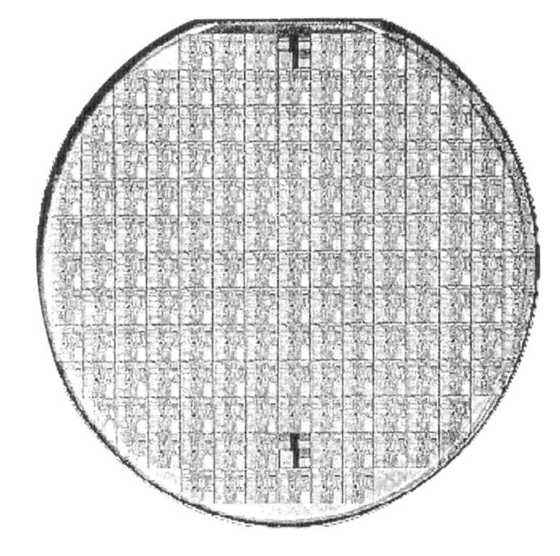

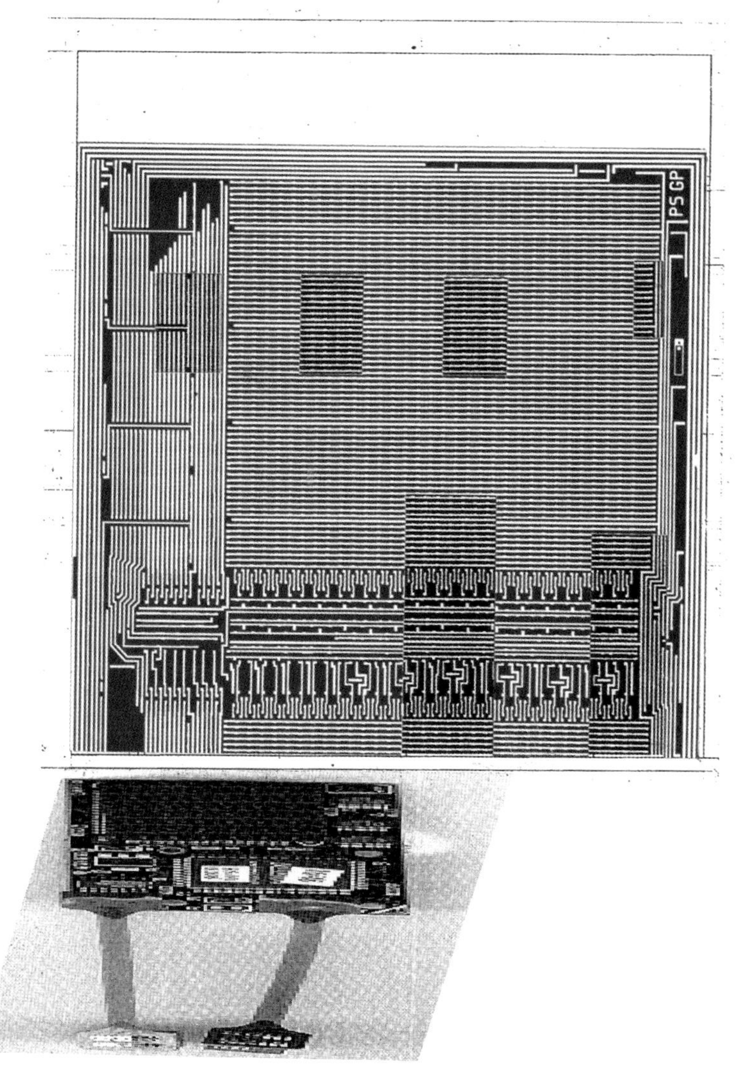

M I/A C R O
(33 : XI)

A macro-version of the silicone microchip covers the wall of The Museum. The micro surface recalling macro situations - aerial city views and giant architectures like the Forbidden City of Peking - is here placed upon the 'meso' scale of The Museum's wall. MI/ACRO uses actual materials of the information age- copper, sand/silica crystals, silver, etc., which are also materials of more archaic ages.

ref: MOMA Catalog of enlarged chips

Mi/zcro

An important part of our mission statement reads "... to bring to public notice outstanding examples of human artistry & ingenuity on the microscopic scale." In attempt to fulfill this mandate the Museum has in the recent past offered two exhibitions "Nanotechnology – Machines in the Microscopic Realm," an exhibition which brought together & presented the extraordinary efforts of perhaps a dozen individuals working at a handful of institutions around the country & the world to develop motors, gears, springs, sensors & other contrivances, all in the scale of the diameter of a human hair.

"The Eye of the Needle – The Unique World of Microminiatures of Haggop Sandaldjian," an exhibition currently on display at the Museum presents the complete work of this Armenian microminiaturist. Sandaldjian in the last 10 years of his life created some 33 remarkable sculptures carved from single strands of human hair ranging from Pope John Paul II to Snow White & the Seven Dwarfs, which, mounted in the eyes of needles & all but invisible to the unaided eye, reveal astonishing detail when viewed through a microscope eye piece.

LARGE AS LIFE,
or
GREAT BIG
(34 : XII)

From Egypt LARGE AS LIFE, or GREAT BIG 'imports' at full scale a piece of the portico of the temple at Esna (also known as Latopolis), including a Lotus column from the hypostyle. The size of the Temple in Egypt is literally set against the size of The Museum. The scale of ancient Egypt is also set against the scale of Los Angeles and Venice Boulevard today. Because the temple is too big (it is, in fact, Great Big) to fit in and on The Museum, it is cropped and truncated, appearing as it did for many years in the post-ancient town of Esna prior to the excavation that revealed its lower parts. An illusion of immense depth would be created in the space behind the column, leading one to imagine an infinite and mysterious space beyond. An illusionistically deep space would also occur at the ground surface, where the 'big as life' column dives into the ground, causing us to wonder how far down it goes. It might dive into a line of marshy grass or planted papyrus. Two doors would lead to the interior, one made out of the hieroglyphic wall segment, and the other made into the infinitely deep space of the intercolumniation.

ref: Susan Stewart's *On Longing*- essay on the Miniature and the Gigantic
ref: *Monuments of Egypt: the Napoleonic Editions*
ref: Boulee and Ledoux's shadowed space, esp. as described by Tony Vidler

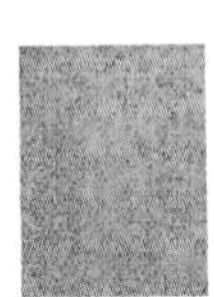

Large as Life or
Great Big

Issues of scale have, for a variety of reasons, held a particular interest for us at the Museum. Scale has played an important role in a great many of the Museum's exhibitions — not only in the ~~most~~ more ~~[illegible]~~ obvious cases where issues of scale are at the center of the exhibition such as "Nanofickology" & "The Eye of the Needle" but also in many other of the Museum's exhibits such as "Megalo[illegible] Foetens" which relates the curious symbiotic ~~[illegible]~~ that centers on the relationship between an unusually large ant & a microscopic fungal spore.

A number of years ago the Museum presented an exhibition of three-dimensional miniature complete w/ cataptric projections which recreated a selection of 16th century miniatures, paintings from the 'Balls Hours', a book of hours. Similarly the compare & contrast environment created by the presentation of miniature Sonnabend study along side the full scale recreation of the same study casts light on issues of scale.

Still, clearly most of the Museum's ventures into the realm of scale have been in the direction of the diminutive. Perhaps out of constraints imposed by financial & space limitations or perhaps out of a basic philosophical predilection, at the MJT we are drawn to & have placed in public view the minute, the smaller than life, in contrast to other of our institutional sisters the missions of which encompass placing in view examples of the greater end of the scale spectrum.

MEMNON #1
(35 : XII)

As in LARGE AS LIFE, or GREAT BIG, MEMNON wall for The Museum plays out the imported gigantic against the local middle scale. This time, the gigantic is literally the giant - the Colossus of Memnon from Egyptian Thebes. In keeping with the mythic tale - that the statue produced musical sounds when touched by the morning rays of sun - the front wall of The Museum would sound at the hour that sun first hits it. Entering The Museum would mean passing between the spread feet of Memnon, through the body-shaped cut of the small attendant posed there in the stone base. Changeable text and the words 'The Museum of Jurassic Technology' (written especially large) would be scribed upon the legs, following the model of the inscriptions made by the Emperor Hadrian and others along foot, ankles, shins, and knees of the Colossus. A slot in the wall would give way to a gargantuan view, in this case, Fischer von Erlach's depiction of Babylon. It could also give a view across the plains and ecologies of Los Angeles as if we had moved up to the eye level of Memnon to overlook it. The toes of Memnon might protrude in order to make places to sit.

ref: Wonder's of the Ancient World
ref: *Monuments of Egypt: The Napoleonic Editions*
ref. Nero's Colossus moved with 34 elephants and 80' high scaffolding by Emperor Hadrian and converted to a sun god

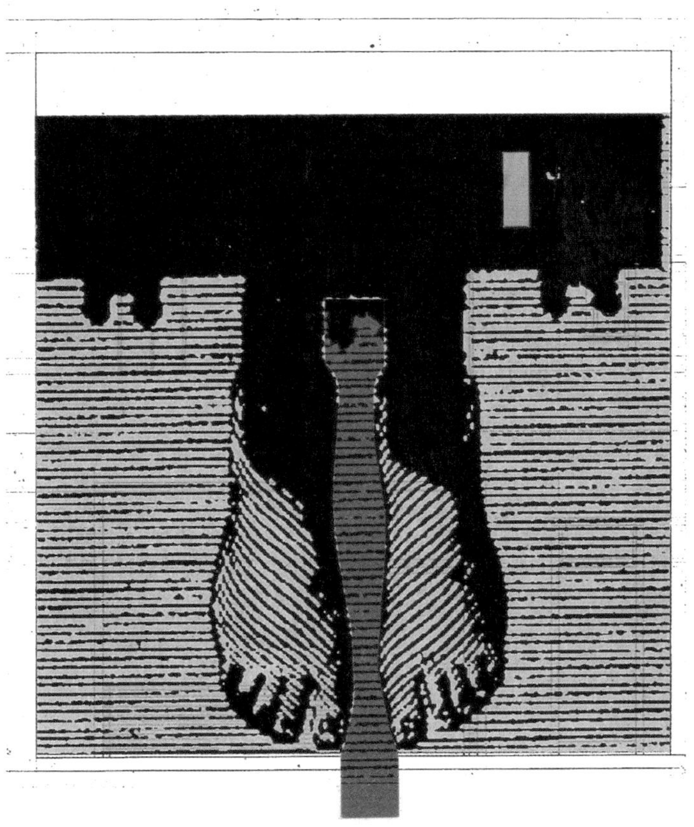

MEMNON #2
(36 : XII)

Following upon the story of MEMNON #1, MEMNON #2 also makes an entrance between the spread feet of the Colossus, but this time we enter between the feet of the reclining giant. A slot in the wall would give way to a view of a place nearby where Memnon's head would have come to rest, if he were all there.

ref: Fragments of the Colossal Statue of Constantine sitting in the courtyard of the Capitoline Museum in Rome (photograph)

XIII

37
XIII

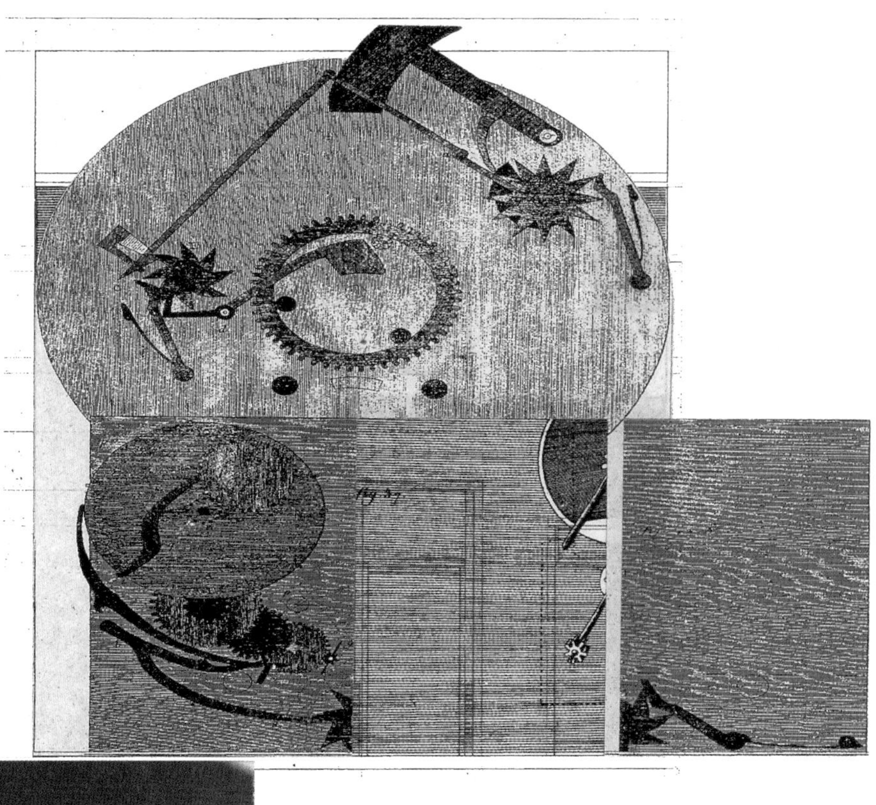

RECORDING INSTRUMENT
(37 : XIII)

The building becomes a probe, gauge, receiver, recorder, record, and container of records of information about its micro environment. The wall (front end of the apparatus) displays the instruments. Conditions that might be measured and recorded include weather data of all kinds, traffic conditions, air chemistry, sky/atmosphere conditions via mirror, sounds from the streets, elevated views through a periscope, changing events in front of the museum projected via camera obscura, visitors to the museum, and sun 'movement' (earth rotation). The instruments would be quite real. Their existence on the surface of the wall, through emphasis and perhaps exaggeration, form the very composition of the facade. All of the readouts and records are kept on the opposite surface (the inside of the wall), where the participant is able to survey the immediate (not past or future) world excluded by the wall of the Museum. The readouts grouped inside might evoke a control room: dim, a low hum, oscillating registers, blinking data. They would form the threshold for the reentrance to the outside world.

ref: Recording instruments (telescopes, weather balloons) that take in data only to reveal this information in some remote place.

READOUT
(38 : XIII)

The wall as instrument here is designed to give immediate readouts of useful or useless information captured again from the immediate surroundings. The instruments, in exaggerated form record and display (readout) concerning a variety of situations. The participant might be counted on a daily, weekly, or yearly basis, and this information indicated as a kind of scale. The weight of the participant might be measured (during transgression of the wall (entrance/exit), and the marking of the weight shown by a very large recording needle. In ways similar to RECORDING INSTRUMENT, information about the sun, wind, sound, activity (people, vehicles) would be made visible in an exaggerated form. One version of this 'device' stations recording devices at points around the city (or world), and the information is relayed via modem and indicated again in the exaggerated movement of various readout systems (hands on a dial, sliding scales, expanding and contracting shapes, etc.). The composition of the wall is in flux, but in flux against a fixed background structure that helps to clarify the readings (thus grid and other scaling systems). One beautiful recording part of this wall of readouts might be the exaggerated movement of a marker due to the earth's movement (earthquakes). A camera would be positioned to record these events, allowing playback for those not present during these events.

ref: Weigh stations for trucks
ref: Wind socks at airports
ref: Chinese seismic instruments

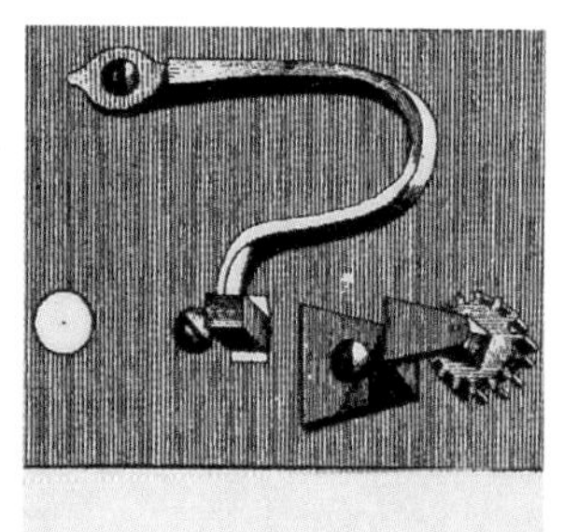

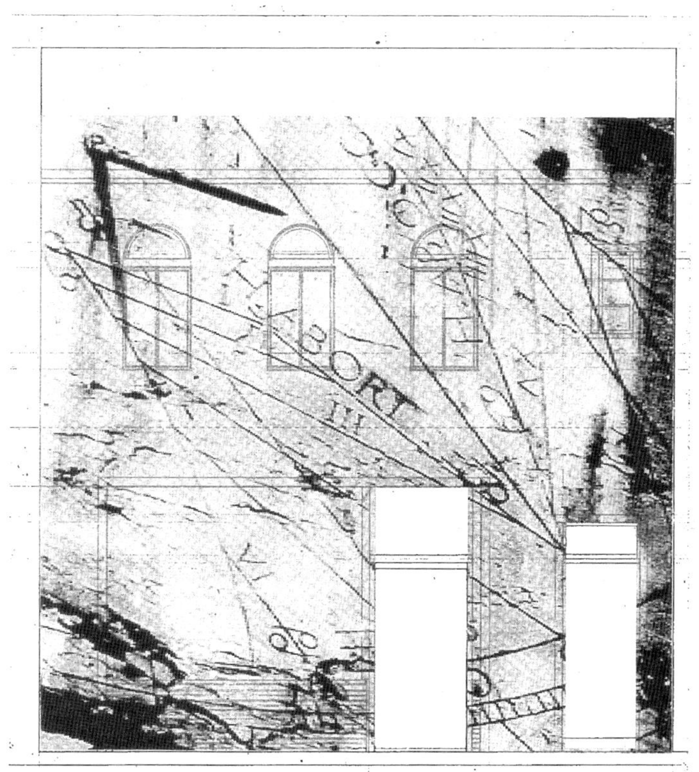

SHADOW CHASER
(39 : XIII)

In the tradition of the wall mounted sun dial used in Greek and Roman times (and probably Egyptian and other early civilizations), the whole wall is formulated to be the 'shadow chaser' or time keeper. The wall is probably constructed quite simply, perhaps smooth stucco, with a slight curve to mark the time of day when the sun leaves the surface. The wall might also be tilted slightly more to the south, and tilted some from being perpendicular to the earth's surface. A tilted part might extend from the top of the wall and would keep a constant angle to the midday sun. Various Gnomons and other shadow casting devices would form the beginning of the composition. The completion of the composition would always be the shadows cast by these devices. Thus, the façade would have many distinct compositions of lines and shapes, depending on the time of day, season, and lighting intensity. The wall would also cast shadows from the moon, from fixed lighting along Venice Boulevard, and from passing cars at night. If successful, the viewer standing in front of SHADOW CHASER would have the sensation that the earth is rotating. Certain of the shadow markings might allow a reading of daily time, calendar time, and seasonal time. The 17,000 year wobble of the earth might also be marked. As an added complication, the wind might be allowed to contaminate the recording, with the gnomons being quite fragile and wind sensitive, thus allowing the lines of the wall to move quickly at times.

ref: Gnomon devices from Greek and Roman times
ref: Window grill in Tarquinia that casts a mysterious shadow on a wall
ref: Wall of Palazzo Te where the early morning sun forms one pattern, and the midday sun forms another pattern on one particular south facing wall.

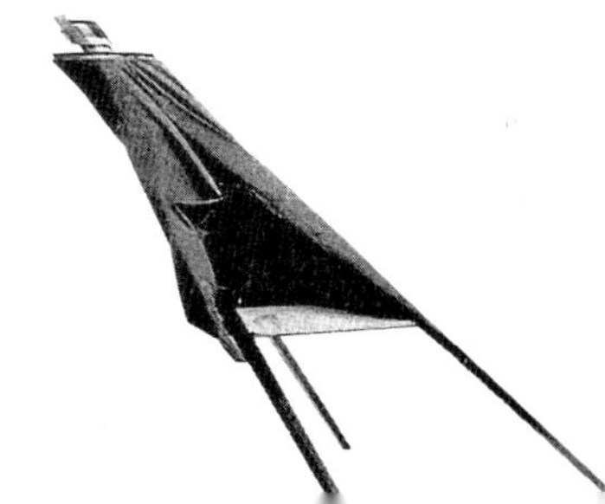

XIV

40
XIV

Layers. #1

1. Bologna facade
ideas of past
cut off.
a. historical
2. magnification of
3. Depths
4. Giotto facade
Minoan facade

LAYERS OF REINHABITATION
(40 : XIV)

Layers of Inhabitations appear on the wall of The Museum. In this case, a piece of Alberti's Palazzo Rucellai, a piece collected from the history of architecture, is re-inhabited by The Museum. The base is marked with the diagonal lines of 'Opus Reticulatum'- first seen in ancient Roman construction, then quoted as a scratched-in and magnified version by Alberti, and now seen here in its third appearance in architecture (at one further step of magnification) on the wall of The Museum. Other contaminations proceed and follow the Alberti superimposition.

ref: Leon Battista Alberti
ref: Piazza di Santo Stefano, Bologna (photo)

Layers of Reinhabitation

Even though young by comparison w/ many institutions, The Museum of Jurassic Technology has in less than a century woven a substantial & substantially layered history of its own. Beginning in the 1910's w/ the collecting activities of the Thomas & the subsequent & questionable transfer of the collections to Gerard Billius, his loss of interest & the associated decay of the artifacts & finally the Cannon donation to the MJT in the 1980's the museum & its collections have already attained a complexly layered historical composition.

Beyond Belief: The Museum as Metaphor

Ralph Rugoff

The Museum of Jurassic Technology is situated between Los Angeles's east and west sides, sandwiched between a realty office and a now-defunct forensic laboratory. Modest in scale though not in ambition, it calls itself 'an ethnographic and natural history museum of the lower Jurassic,' designed to serve both the academic community and the general public.

Its exhibition spaces, cluttered with traditional glass-and-wood vitrines, form a dimly lit maze. Displays feature preserved insects, animal skeletons, dioramas, mineralogical specimens, and various science and technology exhibits - some obsolete, like the Boules of Conundrum, a brass mechanism for producing man-made gems, others covering more recent material such as 'Life in the Extreme Ultraviolet' and 'Post-Plasmatic Visualization.' Many of these displays utilize up-to-date viewer-activated and audiovisual technologies, but under the direction of founder David Wilson, the museum has taken great pains to create the impression of having nineteenth-century roots.

Presentations are reassuringly meticulous. Fact-filled wall labels offer scholarly, step-by-step explanations for even the oldest natural phenomena, enacting the museum's mission of guiding viewers 'from familiar objects toward the unfamiliar.' In those exhibits that feature an audio component, the narrator speaks in a tone familiar from countless educational films: pedantic, slightly pompous, void of ambiguity. Occasionally you come across blank wall spaces and empty vitrines occupied by signs reading: 'Exhibit temporarily removed for study,' indicating that the curatorial and research staffs are on the ball.

On the surface of it, this isn't a museum with which you could fall in love. Yet as you make your way through its dimly lit halls, a vaguely disturbing thought arises - like a faint scratching at a back window of the mind. While this is supposedly a Museum of Jurassic Technology, there are few displays that actually make reference to either the geographic Jurassic (the area of the lower Nile) or the prehistoric time period. Most exhibits seem to deal with science or natural history, but a significant number venture outside this sphere in presenting fruit-stone carvings, fifteenth-century battle maps, and engravings of the Tower of Babel. An animated model of Noah's Ark and several references to a higher power - the introductory slide show ends with the line 'Glory to Him, Who endureth forever' - stir up suspicions that this may not, after all, be a secular institution.

Taken together, these observations lead to an irrevocable conclusion: the museum isn't what it says it is. If not an outright impostor, at the very least it has to be considered an unreliable narrator. Of course, this quality of being hard to pin down, of suggesting there's more than meets the eye here, is essential to seduction. More than one romance has begun on exactly this kind of shaky ground, and such is the terrain on which my own relationship with this institution blossomed.

The Delani and Sonnabend Hall, located in the rear of the MJT, is its most lyrical installation, and may even be a type of love story, though one where the protagonists never meet. Through a series of exhibits and listening stations, it chronicles the lives and work of two individuals from the early twentieth century: Madalena Delani, a classical singer afflicted with what may have been Korsakoff Syndrome (which impairs short-term memory), and Geoffrey Sonnabend, supposedly a professor of neurophysiology at Northwestern University.

Skipping over the wealth of biographical detail provided in the exhibit, I will cut to the chase: in 1936 Delani gives a concert in a Brazilian spa resort near the giant Iguaçu Falls. Sonnabend is also at the spa, convalescing from a breakdown suffered after an unsuccessful research project on the memory pathways of carp. After attending Delani's recital of romantic *lieder*, the professor from Illinois spends a sleepless night, during which he devises a novel theory of memory. He spends the next eight years elaborating this theory, finally publishing his findings in a three-volume tome titled *Obliscence, Theories of Forgetting, and the Problem of Matter*, which is synopsized in the museum's Hall of Obliscence.

Departing from previous research in the field, Sonnabend maintained that forgetting, rather than remembering, is the inevitable outcome of all experience. In other words, we are all amnesiacs, and what we know as 'memory' is nothing more than an imaginative act scaffolded around decaying fragments of lived experience. Memory, Sonnabend wrote, is only a confabulation designed to 'buffer us against the intolerable knowledge of the irreversible passage of time and the irretrievability of its moments and events.' Did Delani's singing, which one critic reportedly described as 'steeped in a haunting sense of loss,' somehow inspire Sonnabend's theory? Was her plaintive vocal expression due to her lost connection to the past? In a darkened chamber of reliquaries that is the exhibit's most poetic installation, the singer's biography is recounted by a voice-over narration that drops hints along these lines.

To the accompaniment of Delani's singing, the viewer is led through a rise-and-fall career biography that underscores the limits of documentary reconstruction. Wall-mounted photographs showing the singer at progressive stages of her career are illuminated at appropriate moments, but quite unlike the visuals we expect from historical documentaries. The information they provide is negligible. Similarly, the personal effects displayed in vitrines - concert programs, opera gloves, sheet music - add little to our understanding of Delani's fate. The viewer is left to mull over a grim coda that has the irony of an O'Henry twist: after giving the concert at the Iguaçu Falls, the singer returned to Buenos Aires the next day and was killed in a car crash. The concert Sonnabend heard was her last.

Is this a true story? You can never be sure at the MJT, where a number of exhibits - such as a display devoted to a South American bat that uses radar to fly through solid walls - strain credulity. Even when the suspicion arises that fact and fiction have been deftly intermingled, it remains difficult to delineate their respective borders. By making use of information that lies on the edges of our cultural literacy - things we've heard of but don't necessarily know much about, such as bat radar, ultraviolet rays, or the Jurassic itself - the museum draws us into a shadowy zone where exhibits slip from the factual to the metaphorical with disarming fluency. It is this fluency which makes the seduction irresistible.

*　　　*　　　*

It's difficult to characterize an exhibit like the Delani and Sonnabend Hall. On one level, it's a rumination on twists of fate, and the convergence of inexplicable lines of influence. On another, the lugubrious Delani exhibit, which concludes with a glowing photograph of the forgotten singer's headstone, could be a memorial to memory itself.

But for a history museum to pay serious attention to a theory that holds all knowledge of the past as an illusion - clearly this is a loaded proposition. In fact it's hard not to see the Delani and Sonnabend Hall as a commentary on the larger institution, calling attention to the aura of unreality surrounding its own recreations (such as Sonnabend's attic study). It might also be a dig at museums in general, which - as repositories of cultural memory built around 'decaying fragments of experience' - conform to Sonnabend's theory of memory as imaginative reconstruction.

In the end, there's no way of knowing how to read this material. Like other smitten lovers, I have visited and revisited the museum only to find myself seduced again. I look for clues wherever I can, even in the museum's stationery, where one finds the motto *Ut translatio natura* - Latin for 'nature as metaphor,' an idea echoing religious and Romantic concepts of nature as a text to be translated, the scene of hidden meanings.

A diorama on the Cameroonian Stink Ant (officially known as Megaloponera foetens) may or may not embody this idea. Through the narration track, we learn that the occasional Stink Ant, while foraging for food along the rain forest floor, inhales a microscopic fungus spore, which, once seated in the ant's tiny brain, begins to grow at an accelerated rate. The afflicted ant soon appears troubled and confused, and for the first time in its life, leaves the forest floor and begins to climb a vine or plant. At a prescribed height, it impales itself onto the stalk. Within two weeks, a bright orange spike emerges front the ant's ravaged body, dropping new spores onto the forest floor for other unsuspecting ants to inhale.

Unless you're a tropical entomologist, it's hard to know whether this is the story of a real ant, or a parable of all-consuming obsession. It might well be both. The tale of the Stink Ant could also be an allegory for what happens to many of the MJT's visitors: exposed to the museum's exhibits, they initially become troubled and confused, but eventually persuade others to visit in order to be infected by this same experience. The idea of the exhibit-as-metaphor opens a veritable can of worms, partly because metaphor is malleable. Rather than conveying ready-to-digest information, the exhibits unsettle us with information about information. The artifacts we're supposed to be learning about start to dematerialize into a field of questions about display and the nature of knowledge.

One result is that the general parameters of what constitutes all exhibit grow fuzzy. On coming out into the lobby, it's easy to wonder whether the gift store is yet another exhibit, and perhaps even the brass plaque engraved with the names of the museum's supposed founders. Might not these displays also harbor veiled commentaries, something to do with the way contemporary museums increasingly exist for their merchandising operations and the aggrandizement of benefactors?

The suspicion that these exhibits are metaphorical induces minor paranoia. Of course a little paranoia goes a long way toward shaking up habitual perceptions. In certain cases, the uncertainty that the MJT instills in a viewer can produce what I call Stoned Thinking. When I refer to the Stoner, you may imagine someone poring over the cover of a rock album, decoding cryptic messages and its previously unconsidered cosmic implications. But the Stoner's rapture speaks of an experience of total involvement and immanent distraction, not unlike what we see in Vermeer's *Astronomer*. It's something close to a trance.

The effect of Stoned Thinking is to scramble our perception of boundaries, so that almost anything looms as a potential exhibit deserving an intimate once-over. To give an example, a friend once emerged from the exhibition halls and started examining an unusual object on the front desk - what he assumed was some kind of antiquated seismic instrument. Upon inquiring, he learned it was a tape dispenser temporarily out of tape.

The Stoner's fascinated gaze is also akin to the lover's regard for the beloved, which obliterates the rest of the world with its laser focus. A great part of love's maintenance is earned by paying close attention, and keeping this attentive vision alive. Inasmuch as it produces a similar gaze, I find the MJT to be a deeply romantic museum. Instead of asking us to suspend disbelief, it leads viewers beyond belief. It's not that it aims to discredit rational scholarship; rather it embraces its rhetoric as a peculiar and distinctive voice, but by no means a definitive one. The museum never discards categories such as history and fiction, or science and art; it simply implies they're not necessarily hygienic, that contagion and overlap between them is possible, if not actually quite common. It's a principle at work in the museum's own multiple identity. On leaving, visitors may wonder whether it's a real museum or a simulation, a science museum or an art installation? If it harkens back to the curiosity collections of the eighteenth and nineteenth centuries, can it also be a modern meta-museum - a museum about museology?

In accommodating contradictions and allowing for the existence of parallel systems of thought and parallel realities, the museum seems to be in agreement with the increasingly popular notion that historical perspective is relative. This staple of postmodern thinking has been turning up in all kinds of museums, but with an important difference. For the sake of comparison, I will consider a couple of examples.

First: Los Angeles's fifty-four-million-dollar Gene Autry Museum dedicated to exhibiting and interpreting the heritage of the West. At times, the Autry seems bent on charting the histories of all possible Wests - of the geographic area from Mississippi to California as well as the various Wests of popular imagination, spanning Frederic Remington and Buffalo Bill to Bonanza and the Marlboro Man.

In more than one exhibit, the museum stresses a relativist approach to history. In the Spirit of Discovery gallery, we learn of diverse cultural groups 'who discovered the West in their own time period,' including Vietnamese refugees who 'discovered' California in the late l970s. Elsewhere, a diagram of the OK Corral showdown drawn by Wyatt Earp is accompanied by a note that this shouldn't be mistaken for an impartial account since it only represents the victors' viewpoint. This relativist philosophy also informs the museum's equal treatment of historical fact and Hollywood fabrication. The Autry's curatorial premise, baldly stated, runs something like this: since much of what we know of the west derives from media imagery, these inventions are as much a part of the legacy as real events. Complicating matters, references to the historical West are irremediably tainted by myth and popular media. A knowing display-text accompanying a Billy the Kid mannequin concludes: 'Myth overwhelmed fact, and today, no one knows the real Billy.'

At the Autry, as at many more progressive museums, we're told that the history we encounter there isn't definitive, yet the museum's own authority remains unquestioned. Despite all this relativist posturing, the underlying politics of our viewing approach remain unchanged; we are looking for the truth. By contrast, the MJT places its very authenticity in doubt - not just the authenticity of what it exhibits. It does so not simply by mixing fact and fiction - an approach that isn't inherently subversive by any means. At the Museum of Jurassic Technology, duplicity is used as means of instruction, not as a way to bolster its authority. In a society where the line between news and entertainment is increasingly blurred, its labyrinth of confusion offers a canny reflection of what has actually become our daily experience of shuffling fact and fiction. If knowledge is power, then an awareness of the tenuousness of knowledge can only make us suspicious of how power is wielded.

Consider the Los Angeles County Sheriff's Museum, located in Whittier, California: this museum interweaves documentary and fantasy, but to a very different end. Outside its front entrance near the Sheriff's Training Academy, a restored patrol car - a modified 1976 Chevy Nova - is displayed along with a text describing it as a 'mystical vehicle.' Inside the museum, a giant vitrine of confiscated occult objects includes tarot cards, a Motley Crue banner, a press release from Anton S. LaVey's Church of Satan, and a variety of plastic dashboard saints. As a corollary to the occult section, several exhibits canonize the chief of the department, Sheriff Sherman Block. As if testifying to his supernatural election, one vitrine features a charred section of fuselage taken from an airplane hit by lightning while Sheriff Block was on board. Elsewhere, photographs depict the Sheriff 's meetings with the Pope and Santa Claus. Now clearly no Chevy Nova, even one with a heavy-duty radiator, is a mystical vehicle; nor is the occult a major cause of crime in Los Angeles; nor is Sheriff Block anybody's candidate for sainthood. Here the mixture of fact and fiction is a consequence not of radical doubt but something more like radical certainly. It's used to create a mythical image of the department in which sheriffs appear as Christian crusaders battling Satan's legions; transcending Civic issues, law enforcement is presented as part of an eternal battle of Good against Evil.

From another viewpoint, though, the Museum of Jurassic Technology reads as a metaphor for the fallible self, especially our capacity for unconsciously fusing real events with made-up ones - in memory as well as present time. But this museum isn't merely a model of something else - it's a technology for altering habitual ways of seeing and thinking. Abrogating its own authority is central to this process. In puncturing its institutional facade, it frees us from feeling beholden to the museum's traditional 'objectivity,' and opens the way to our recovering the authority of subjective experience.

In visiting the MJT, you go in ready to hold up your end of the bargain, only to find that thinking as usual doesn't work here. By subtly breaching our customary contract with museums, the MJT lures us into the process of forging a new one - and to experiencing point of view as a point of negotiation. Whereas the Gene Autry Museum tells us that history is made up of contending, but essentially stable, viewpoints, the Jurassic problematizes the very notion of point of view. One result is the radical reorientation that I call Stoned Thinking. The implication isn't that other museums are necessarily bogus, but that the meaning of any exhibit is open to negotiation because the museum isn't merely a place that preserves culture - it's involved in the process of inventing it in a deal worked out with each and every visitor.

The architect Louis Kahn once complained that most museums are so fatiguing that the first thing you want on entering is a cup of coffee. I think one wants that cup of coffee because so many museum exhibits attract our attention only to immobilize our curiosity. Their atmosphere of infallible authority is paralyzing. The deal they offer leaves little room for negotiation. The visitor, like the objects cluttering the museum's halls, is locked in an airless space.

Where there's no room for playful negotiation, there's no chance for seduction. As with any romance, once the negotiation process goes stale, the relationship is as good as dead. In working out a deal with its visitors, the MJT embodies a mischievous generosity. When it disorients and confuses us, it does so only to re-present this capacity as something infinitely valuable; it leaves us with the feeling that questions are worth holding onto as aesthetic acts, and that uncertainty is a key part of pleasure. In place of an encounter with profundity and depth, it offers an experience of an endless - because always changing - surface.

* * *

As I've noted, this museum mixes things - like religion and science, history and art - that are supposed to be kept apart. The very idea of law, on the other hand, is founded on the principle of separation. In ancient Greek, the original meaning of nomos, the law, is that which is divided up into parts.

From a psychoanalytic viewpoint, the museum might then conceivably represent what French analyst Janine Chasseguet-Smirgel calls 'the perverse solution' - a forging of a hybridized vision through the dissolving of accepted boundaries. It's a vision that tempts us to replace a love of truth with a taste for sham.

The perversity of the MJT, though, is that it uses falsehoods as a way of conveying a type of experiential truth that escapes analytical approaches. In this light, it corresponds to what contemporary Italian philosopher Gianni Vattimo has called 'weak thought' - a mode of reflection that stands in contrast to a metaphysics that is universalizing, domineering, and self-centered. Weak thought explores experiences of 'diffused significance,' approaching its subjects with a mix of nostalgia, supplication, tenuousness, and a respect for its own frailties.

Likewise, the MJT's curatorial policy is characterized by a tender regard for the frail, the pathetic, and the neglected. The word curator derives from the Latin to 'care for,' and here caretaking extends not simply to objects, but to our relationship with the past, particularly those portions that have been overlooked, dismissed, forgotten, or destroyed (as supposedly were parts of its own collection during the great wars). Here a home is provided for the marginal artifact, for things not usually prized or deemed worthy of serious display.

In the museum's Library for the Diffusion of Useful Information, an exhibit features letters sent to the Mount Wilson Observatory near the turn of the century by people wishing to explicate their own often highly personal cosmological theories to the observatory's astronomers. (It's worth noting that the experimental basis for the theory of relativity was developed at this same observatory). These letters, however farfetched, call to mind the proverbial 'path not taken,' and stand in for all endeavors that for whatever reason wander outside accepted paradigms. To the hubris of scientific certainty, they offer a hint of the way false data and experimental accidents often lead an individual off the beaten path and on to significant discoveries.

Which is why, speaking as someone who doesn't like to be pigeon-holed or labeled, I wouldn't mind being an exhibit in the Museum of Jurassic Technology. This may sound like an odd idea. Being put on a pedestal conventionally implies an uncomfortable alienation. To be made into an exhibit means suffering a metaphysical abduction, a not-so-latent violence.

This view was made poignantly clear to me at a panel I recently attended in Los Angeles on the legacy of the Black Panther Party. The organizer of the panel had dug up a collection of Panther graphics from the I960s and early '70s, and had covered a wall with once-familiar posters of power salutes and heavily armed Panther leaders. One of the speakers, a former Panther, looked over at the wall and remarked that he felt like he was in a museum. It was a bittersweet statement: the price of seeing his own history enshrined as a museum piece was his present dislocation from ongoing political dialogue.

If a museum can disrupt our sense of distance from the objects it displays, it might not serve to isolate the past so much as to link it to our current experience. So as a living subject with a history still in the process of unfolding, I wouldn't be terribly worried - if I were to become an exhibit at the Jurassic - that visitors would walk away feeling sure they knew my entire story I would be an exhibit whose truth one could only appeal to, but never possess. It is precisely the feeling of possession that is so fatal to romance. Deciding whether or not you'd care to be on exhibit in a given institution may not be such an unreasonable criteria for evaluating the deals museums offer us. Wherever you can display yourself without fear of being summarily judged, there's a chance for lasting romance.

Notes

David Wilson

The following are notes prepared by David Wilson, Director of The Museum of Jurassic Technology, in response to the Wrapper drawings.

Dear Robert and Mary-Ann,

Here at embarrassingly long last, is a pale response to your extraordinary outpouring of thoughts and ideas occasioned by the refurbishing of the front of 9341 Venice Blvd.

Most of these thoughts were written during the trip I took recently with Ralph Rugoff to Kiev and St. Petersburg - both extraordinary and wonderful places. I hope these responses prove to be of some use. I am not certain how much closer any of this will bring us to improving the sheer strength of 9341 Venice Blvd., but I have enjoyed the process a great deal nonetheless.

I had some other thoughts about the building itself that I would like to pass along but think I should get this material to you now.

I unfortunately did not respond to all of your thoughts but just those that seemed to resonate immediately with our work here at the Museum. Let me know if any or all of this makes any sense to you. I wrote all of this material by hand as we traveled from place to place but on returning and rereading the thoughts, I wanted to clean up and rewrite a bit. If you would like me to write this material again by hand, I would be happy to do so. In addition if you need further responses please let me know. I would be happy to try to write more.

Many thanks again for all of this.

Sincerely.

David

ARK
I : 1

Since our inception, the image of the Ark has been and continues to be central to the Museum of Jurassic Technology from many points of view:

The Ark of Noah as the first and most complete museum of natural history the world has ever known. The Ark as the most complete and perfect form of the museum as an encyclopedic endeavor - one (or in this case two) of every living thing.

An institution that has been very influential in the formation of our Museum was grounded in the collecting efforts of John Tradescant, *a 17th century botanist who in the course of his botanical gatherings also amassed a large collection of rarities and artifacts from many and varied places which were then categorized in an idiosyncratic fashion*, who exhibits his varied and often idiosyncratic artifacts under the name of "Tradescant's Ark" *in South Lambeth. This collection was (under questionable circumstances) subsequently deeded to Elias Ashmole, a barrister, who on his death donated the collections to Oxford University, thereby creating that museum which even today bears his name.*

Our Museum's foundation collection was donated by Mary Rose Cannon of Pasadena, California *in 1978.* Mary Cannon *had inherited the collection from her (adopted) grandfather Gerard Billius who had, in turn* received the collection *in the 1950's* from a gardener *named Owen Thum, whose father (also named Owen Thum) had, in the decade of the 1910's and 1920's, drawn together this curious collection of artifacts and memorabilia primarily from areas surrounding his home in South Platt, Nebraska, where for over a decade beginning in 1927 he* exhibited the collections in an abandoned schoolhouse under the name of "Thum's Ark".

Noah and his wife as early, possibly the first, collector (in August '96, the Museum is scheduled to open an exhibition entitled "Los Angeles' Hidden Collectors", which will place in public view the collections of a number of Los Angeles area mobile home dwellers while tracing the lineage of the automobile trailer and mobile home to Noah's Ark).

CONTAINER / CRATE / CHEST
I : 2
Extraordinary amounts of thought, time, and effort go into the creation of containers or crates for the Museum's artifacts - vibration dampening, acid free, temperature sensitive temporary homes for the objects in question. Almost mobile museums in and of themselves, the purpose of the container or crate is to protect and preserve during this a most trying and danger fraught period for any artifact - transportation.

DISPLAY CASE
II : 6

Objects change dramatically when placed under glass. Artifacts contained within vitrines are inaccessible, unreachable. Objects sequestered in such a manner are possessed of enhanced desirability - implied value. A well designed and constructed display case places the contained object in a parallel and apparently timeless reality.

State of the art display cases with light, temperature, humidity, and even the constituent parts of atmosphere under precise control place the objects contained in the case literally in another reality - a purer almost eternal reality where, mercifully spared from the ravages of time, objects can survive, like the uncorruptables, perhaps forever.

CASES II : Reflections
II : 6

A darkened room full of intensely lit display cases provides a tangle of reflection. We have greatly framed ourselves to see objects and not their reflections, however if we allow ourselves to see what is actually there, the environment is far more complex. Objects float in space while others exist in vitrines from one perspective and disappear from another - two or more objects can share the same physical space and their numbers can be multiplied infinitely. From the perspective of the Museum's patron, each of these objects, unverifiable by physical contact, is as real as the next.

DRAWN OUT / UNDER CONSTRUCTION
V : 14

The task of providing to the world a Museum with minimal staff and a few often desperate if desperately dedicated volunteers is at times overwhelming. New exhibitions, expanded programs, and space renovation are always in the works. Exhibits, many of which employ early 20th or even 19th century technologies have on more than one occasion broken down.

The Museum's exhibitions regularly take longer (often much longer) than anticipated and opening dates are repeatedly pushed back, and finally when opened, certain exhibits within the larger exhibition invariably will be posted with the Museum's all too familiar and well worn "Exhibit Under Construction" signage.

TIME PIECE
VI : 18

Like similar institutions, The Museum of Jurassic Technology itself is a space where standard understandings of time do not apply. It is a place where the past repeats itself over and over - a place where Bernard Maston will time after time succumb to the ravages of influenza - where Geoffery Sonnabend will again and again be struck with the insight that will lead to his "Obliscence Theories of Forgetting and the Problem of Matter" - where Madalena Delani will die hundreds or possibly thousands of untimely deaths in a freak automobile accident while on her way to catch the ferry from Buenos Aires to Montevicleo.

TEXT
VII : 21

The Museum of Jurassic Technology, perhaps more than most institutions, relies on text as a means of sharing what we consider to be indispensable information with patrons and visitors to the Museum.

In earlier days, nearly all of the information accompanying the exhibits was presented by means of text panels. Certain of the Museum's walls became dense with panels of text. Patrons would read through lengthly descriptions and narratives often shifting from one foot to the other to ease the strain of standing for long periods of time required for reading. Benches were provided in hopes of easing the patron's strain; still there came a time when it was clearly untenable to continue to ask patrons, many of whom simply wander in to the Museum off the street, to commit to the amount of reading required to follow the substance of the often complex exhibitions.

Other modes of presenting narrative and descriptions were sought - various forms of recorded presentation including telephone hand-sets and audio-visual offspring. These newer recorded forms of presentation proved to be quite effective - effective not only in providing the Museum's patrons with less labor intensive means of receiving knowledge but effective, in addition, in freeing up valuable wall space within our limited domain for the ever growing body of exhibit materials.

IX : 30
Dear Robert and Mary-Ann,

Here is the second installment. Let me know if there are problems with these.

I have some thoughts about possible ways of proceeding that I will write up and fax you.

Hope all is well.

David

MI/ACRO
XI : 33

An important part of our mission statement reads "... to bring to public notice outstanding examples of human artistry and ingenuity on the microscopic scale." In an attempt to fulfill this mandate the Museum has in the recent past offered two exhibitions "Nanotechnology - Machines in the Microscopic Realm", an exhibition which brought together and presented the extraordinary efforts of perhaps a dozen individuals working at a handful of institutions around the country and the world to develop motors, gears, springs, sensors, and other contrivances, all in the scale of the diameter of a human hair.

"The Eye of the Needle - The Unique World of Microminiatures of Hagop Sandaldjian", an exhibition currently on display at the Museum, presents the complete work of the Armenian microminiaturist. Sandaldjian, in the last 10 years of his life, created some 33 remarkable sculptures carved from single strands of human hair ranging from Pope John Paul II to Snow White and the Seven Dwarfs, which, mounted in the eyes of needles and all but invisible to the unaided eye, reveal astonishing detail when viewed through a microscope eye piece.

Until Hagop Sandaldjian's death in 1990 there were 4 living microminiaturists. We at the Museum were recently fortunate in being able to view the wondrous work of one of the remaining three. Within the wall of a 1100 year old monastery in Kiev is a gallery reminiscent of a set from Tarkofsky's "Solaris" in which Nicoli Syadristy, a Ukranian of perhaps 60 years of age displays 25 of his 80 existing microminiatures. Realized in a variety of media, Syadristy's work varies in subject matter from historic chess games frozen in time on the head of a pin to a portrait of Ernest Hemingway drawn with astonishing detail on a sliced apple seed.

LARGE AS LIFE OR GREAT BIG
XI : 34

Issues of scale have, for a variety of reasons, held a particular interest for us at the Museum. Scale has played an important role in a great many of the Museum's exhibitions - not only in the more obvious cases where issues of scale are at the center of the exhibition, such as "Nanotechnology" and "The Eye of the Needle", but also in many other of the Museum's exhibits such as "Megaloponera foetens" which relates the curious symbiotic tale that centers on the relationship between an unusually large ant and a microscopic fungal spore.

A number of years ago the Museum presented an exhibition of three-dimensional miniatures complete with catoptric projections which revealed a selection of 14th century miniature paintings from the *Belles Heures* - a book of hours. Similarly the compare and contrast environment created by the presentation of the miniature Sonnabend study alongside the full scale recreation of the same study casts light on issues of scale.

Still, clearly most of the Museum's ventures into the realm of scale have been in the direction of the diminutive. Perhaps out of constraints imposed by financial and space limitations or perhaps out of a basic philosophical predelection at the MJT we are drawn to and have placed in public view the minute, the smaller than life, in contrast to other of our institutional sisters, the missions of which encompass placing in view examples of the greater end of the scale spectrum.

LAYERS OF REINHABITATION
XIII : 40

Even though young by comparison with many institutions, The Museum of Jurassic Technology has in less than a century woven a substantial and substantially layered history of its own. Beginning in the 1920's with the collecting activities of the Thums and the subsequent and questionable transfer of the collections to Gerard Billius, his loss of interest and the associated decay of the artifacts and finally the Cannon donation to the MJT in the 1980's, the Museum and the collections have already attained a complexly layered historical composition.

note:
Text in italics is from material forwarded by David on March 11, 1996

Noah's Ark : Plate III : Page 77 : J. Pine Sculp

Essential Bibliography

Lynne Cooke and Peter Wollen, editors
Visual Display: Culture Beyond Appearances
Bay Press
Seattle
1995

Lothar Haselberger
'Deciphering A Roman Blueprint'
Scientific American, June 1995
pp. 84-89

Lothar Haselberger
'The Construction Plans for the Temple of Apollo at Didyma'
Scientific American, December 1985
pp. 126-132

Nicholas Pevsner
'Museums'
A History of Building Types
Princeton University Press
Princeton
1976
pp. 111-138

Ralph Rugoff
Circus Americanus
Verso
London and New York
1995

Essay by Ralph Rugoff
The Eye of the Needle
The Society for the Diffusion of Useful Information
Los Angeles
1996

Susan Stewart
On Longing: Narratives of the Miniature, the Gigantic, the Souvenir, the Collection
Johns Hopkins University Press
Baltimore and London
1993

Sir John Summerson, based on a text by Sir John Soane
A New Description of Sir John Soane's Museum
Trustees of the Museum
London

Anthony Vidler
'Architecture in the Museum'
The Writing of the Walls
Princeton Architectural Press
1987
pp. 165-173

Lawrence Wechsler
Mr. Wilson's Cabinet of Wonder
Pantheon Books
New York
1995

Translated for and edited by Bennet Woodcroft
The Pneumatics of Hero of Alexandria
Taylor Walton & Maberly
1851

Acknowledgments

The Project

We wish to extend our great thanks to:

... Heather Kurze for connecting us with the Museum of Jurassic Technology and David Wilson - we hope that we have lived up to her initial intuitions that Studio Works and the Museum had something to offer one another.

... David Wilson and the Museum of Jurassic Technology for teaching us and strongly reminding us that buildings are often formed less by the conceits, wills, and skills of architects and more through the vital practices of the persons who enact and inhabit them.

... William Hogan, II, for being a most valuable collaborator at Studio Works. He is a person with extraordinary talents who often saved us from being, as he would put it, 'screwed by the pooch'.

The Book

We wish to extend our great thanks to:

... Lars Lerup, for support and friendship of the deepest sort - built through parallel and sometimes intersecting lives of teaching, thinking and making stuff. His commitment to Studio Works and to this book project through Rice University School of Architecture and its Press have been such a boost to us in our work and teaching.

... William Stout, with the help of Dung Ngo, for persevering through a project and for reminding us that bookmaking is as grueling and rewarding as building-making. With his passion for the book, and especially for the design and architecture book, Bill gives us another way through Victor Hugo's 'This Will Kill That' with his proposition that 'This (books) Will Give New Life To That (buildings).

... Pat Morton, working on behalf of the Los Angeles Forum for Art and Architecture, for the energy and content she gave to the book on many fronts - grant writing, organization, publishing, careful and intelligent editing, and for the addition of her essay 'On the Face of It'$_1$.

... Luke Bulman and Kimberly Shoemake, otherwise known as 'thumb', for thumbs definitely NOT sore, but that often stick out and are sometimes green, and also fluorescent orange, psychedelically polka-dot spotted, crushed red velvet, rubber, and other stuff at other times.

... The Los Angeles Forum for Art and Architecture for their support of this publication and for supporting design and architecture in the city of Los Angeles.

... The Graham Foundation for Advanced Studies in the Fine Arts for generously contributing to the publication.

A Coincidence

It should be noted here for posterity the coincidence that produced the titles for Ms. Morton's and Mr. Lerup's texts: 'On the Face of It$_1$', and, 'On the Face of It$_2$'. Both were named by their authors at the same time, in different places, and with no connecting conversations.

A Dedication

To two dear parents whose physical presence was lost during the course of producing this project and this book - Margaret 'Peggy' Barton Mangurian and George Nishan Mangurian. Their spirit lives on in and with us, and we dedicate this book to the living memory we have of them.

Composite photo of façade : Museum of Jurassic Technology : 1995